# IN Her Own Words: The Kim Porter Memoir

# Contents

# INTRODUCTION

Kim Porter was much more than just a beautiful face seen in magazines or music videos. She was a mother, a friend, a supportive partner, and a person who radiated love and grace. From her early days in Columbus, Georgia, to her life in the spotlight of New York and Los Angeles, Kim touched many lives and left an impact that continues to be felt today. While she was known to the public because of her relationships with high-profile figures like Sean "Diddy" Combs, those closest to her knew her as a woman of strength, kindness, and humility.

Kim's journey wasn't without its challenges, but she navigated them with a sense of calm and purpose that inspired everyone around her. She was a private person who didn't seek the limelight for attention, but she handled the public eye with poise. Her priority was always her children, Quincy, Christian, and her twin daughters, D'Lila Star and Jessie James. She cherished her role as a mother, and for her, family was everything.

Her sudden passing in 2018 shocked the world, leaving many to reflect on the life she led and the lessons she left behind. This memoir is not just a retelling of her life's events but a tribute to the grace, love, and wisdom she brought into the world. Through this book, we will explore her journey, from her humble beginnings to her time in the fashion industry, as well as the pivotal role she played behind the scenes in the music world.

## A Childhood of Dreams

Kim Porter's life began in Columbus, Georgia, where she grew up with dreams that far exceeded the boundaries of her small-town environment. From a young age, she wanted to make a name for herself, and it was clear to those who knew her that she had the determination to do just that. In many ways, her upbringing helped mold the strong, compassionate woman she would later become. She learned early on the values of hard work, humility, and perseverance.

Despite her aspirations for the bright lights of big cities, Kim never forgot where she came from. Even as her career blossomed, she remained connected to her roots, often visiting family and old friends in Georgia. This balance between ambition and staying grounded is one of the defining characteristics that those who knew her admired most.

## Entering the Spotlight

After graduating from Columbus High School in 1988, Kim made the bold decision to move to Atlanta, and eventually, to New York City to pursue a career in modelling. The world of fashion is not an easy one to break into, especially as a Black woman in the early '90s. But Kim's persistence paid off. She soon found herself landing opportunities that showcased her beauty and talent on major platforms.

Kim's modelling career was more than just a way to make a living; it was a stepping stone that opened doors to many other opportunities. Whether it was gracing the covers of magazines or walking the runways, she used each opportunity to expand her horizons. But even as she grew in popularity, Kim stayed focused on what truly mattered to her—her family, her friendships, and her sense of self.

## Life of Love and Family

Kim Porter's public life is often associated with her relationships, most notably with Sean "Diddy" Combs. However, her love story began before that with singer Al B. Sure!, with whom she had her first child, Quincy. The bond she shared with her children was unbreakable, and it was clear to anyone who knew her that motherhood was at the core of who she was.

Her relationship with Diddy, while high-profile, was also marked by its deep emotional connection. The two had their ups and downs, but their love endured through the challenges they faced. They shared three children together—Christian and twins D'Lila Star and Jessie James—and despite their separation, Kim and Diddy remained close friends and dedicated co-parents. The way she maintained these relationships with grace and kindness was a testament to the woman she was. Even after parting ways, Kim and Diddy's bond remained a key part of their lives, showing a level of maturity and love that went beyond the usual definitions of relationships.

## A Behind-the-Scenes Influence

While Kim's face may have been familiar due to her modelling work and public appearances, many people didn't realize the significant role she played behind the scenes in the entertainment industry. She wasn't just the partner of a famous music mogul—Kim was a confidante, an advisor, and a source of strength for those around her. She influenced decisions, provided support, and was deeply involved in the creative process of those close to her.

Her presence in the music world, particularly in her support of Diddy's career, was essential, though she never sought credit for it. She preferred to be a quiet force, someone who helped others succeed without needing the spotlight herself. This selflessness was a defining feature of her character and is part of the legacy she left behind.

## The Sudden Loss and Its Impact

When Kim Porter passed away suddenly in November 2018, the world was shocked. At 47, she still had so much life to live and so much more to give. The outpouring of grief from family, friends, and fans was immediate and overwhelming. Diddy's tribute to her as the love of his life and the mother of his children was a raw, emotional reflection of the profound impact she had on him and their family. Tributes poured in from celebrities, friends, and those who had worked with her, all speaking to the incredible person she was.

Her death was not just a loss for her family but for all those who knew and admired her. In the wake of her passing, many began to reflect on how she had touched their lives, whether through personal connections or through her example of how to live with grace and dignity.

## Kim's Enduring Legacy

Kim's legacy continues to live on through her children, who honor her memory in everything they do. Quincy,

Christian, and the twins have all carried forward the lessons their mother taught them, whether in their professional endeavors or in their personal lives. Her influence remains strong, and those who knew her best often speak of how her spirit continues to guide and inspire them.

Through this memoir, we aim to keep Kim Porter's memory alive by sharing her story in a way that honors her legacy and reminds the world of the love, strength, and wisdom she embodied. Her life, though cut short, was a testament to the power of love, resilience, and grace. As we explore the chapters ahead, we will dive deeper into the many facets of Kim Porter's life, learning not just about the public figure, but the woman behind the fame—a woman whose influence will never be forgotten.

# CHAPTER 1

# Growing Up in Georgia

K im Porter's journey began in the small town of Columbus, Georgia, where she was born on December 15, 1970. Growing up in a quiet Southern community, Kim was surrounded by the values of family, faith, and hard work. Her upbringing in Columbus helped shape the strong foundation that guided her through her life, both in the public eye and in her private world.

Columbus, a town known for its rich history and tight-knit community, provided Kim with a sense of security and stability during her early years. It was a place where everyone knew each other, and families were often closely connected. Kim was no different—she was raised in a loving household that instilled strong morals and a desire to achieve big dreams. Her family's support played a significant role in shaping her outlook on life and gave her the courage to chase her ambitions later.

**A Family-Oriented Childhood**

From a young age, Kim was known for her vibrant spirit and infectious smile. Family was everything to her, and this would remain true throughout her life. Her childhood was filled with the love and guidance of her parents, who encouraged her to stay true to herself. Though Columbus was small compared to the major cities where Kim would later live, the town's deep sense of community gave her a firm foundation.

Kim's parents raised her with a sense of responsibility and respect for others, teaching her the importance of humility and kindness. These lessons stayed with her throughout her life, even as she rose to prominence in the entertainment industry. Despite the challenges that come with fame, those who knew Kim often said she never lost her sense of gratitude and grace, which had its roots in her Southern upbringing.

### School Days and Early Aspirations

Kim attended **Columbus High School**, where she was a popular and well-loved student. Her friends often remembered her as someone who stood out—not only for her beauty but also for her warmth and confidence. Even during her school years, Kim had dreams that reached far beyond the borders of her hometown. She would often tell her friends that she was destined for something bigger, and she wasn't afraid to pursue it.

Her time in high school was marked by her interest in the arts, fashion, and entertainment. Kim enjoyed dressing up and was known for her natural style, even as a teenager. Her love for fashion and beauty would later become a central part of her career, but it all began in these early years. Her schoolmates admired her ambition, and teachers often noticed her ability to inspire others.

Despite her dreams of modelling and living in big cities, Kim remained grounded during her time in Columbus. She participated in school activities and formed lifelong friendships with those around her. People who grew up with Kim often recalled that she never acted like she was above anyone. Instead, she treated everyone with kindness, which made her well-liked by her peers.

## Dreams of a Bigger Future

As Kim grew older, it became clear that her aspirations were taking shape. She often talked about moving to a bigger city and becoming a model. Columbus, while a lovely hometown, felt too small for her growing ambitions. Kim was a dreamer, but she was also a doer—she knew that achieving her goals would require hard work and determination. And those who knew her best were confident that she had what it took.

Her decision to leave Columbus after high school wasn't easy. Moving away from her family and the community that had supported her was a difficult step, but Kim understood that her dreams required sacrifices. It was this bold decision that set her on the path to the career and life she would eventually lead.

## A Strong Foundation of Faith

One of the most important influences in Kim's early life was her strong sense of faith. Growing up in the South, attending church and being part of a spiritual community were integral to her upbringing. Kim's faith helped guide her through tough times and provided her with a sense of purpose that would carry her throughout her life. Even in her later years, those close to her often spoke about how grounded she remained in her beliefs.

Faith wasn't just something Kim practiced—it was a core part of who she was. Her spiritual life helped her stay focused and resilient, particularly when she faced challenges in the fast-paced entertainment world. She was known for offering words of encouragement and wisdom to those around her, often reminding others to stay true to their values, just as she had been taught growing up.

## Lessons from Columbus

Though Kim Porter eventually left Columbus to pursue her dreams, she never forgot where she came from. The lessons she learned in her hometown stayed with her throughout her life. Whether it was the importance of humility, the value of hard work, or the power of kindness, Kim carried the spirit of her Southern upbringing with her wherever she went.

Columbus may not have been a large city, but for Kim, it was the perfect place to learn about life, love, and what really mattered. The sense of community, the strength of her family ties, and the faith that was instilled in her from a young age were the building blocks of the remarkable woman she would become. Her time in Columbus laid the foundation for everything she would achieve, and those values shaped her every step.

**The Decision to Move Forward**

By the time Kim graduated from high school, she was ready to take the next step. Her dreams of modelling had grown stronger, and she knew that staying in Columbus would not offer her the opportunities she needed. With the support of her family, she decided to move to Atlanta first, a stepping stone that would later lead her to the modelling world in New York City.

This move marked the beginning of her career, but the core values from her childhood in Columbus would remain with her. Kim knew that no matter where life took her, the lessons she learned growing up would keep her grounded. Columbus gave her more than just a place to call home—it gave her the strength to dream big and the courage to chase those dreams.

# Dreams of Becoming a Model and Moving to Atlanta

Kim Porter's journey toward becoming a model began long before she set foot in the world of fashion. Growing up in Columbus, Georgia, a small town with a tight-knit community, Kim always had a vision for her life that extended beyond the boundaries of her hometown. From a young age, she was fascinated by the glamour of fashion magazines, the runway, and the world of models she saw on television. Her dreams weren't just fantasies; they were a vision she knew she could bring to life with hard work and determination.

Kim's natural beauty was evident to everyone around her, but it wasn't just her looks that set her apart. Even as a teenager, she had a unique sense of style and poise. She carried herself with confidence, something that many noticed early on. Friends and family would often talk about how Kim had the "it factors"—a blend of beauty, elegance, and a strong presence. She wasn't afraid to stand out, and she embraced her individuality in ways that made her feel both strong and beautiful.

As she entered her teenage years, Kim's love for fashion deepened. She spent countless hours poring over fashion magazines, studying models, their poses, and the clothing they wore. She wasn't just looking at the images; she was learning. Kim saw fashion as an art form, a way to express herself and create something that felt true to her identity. She often imagined herself in those glossy pages, walking the runways, and being part of that glamorous world. For Kim, this wasn't a dream far out of reach. She believed it was something she could achieve.

Though she loved her hometown and the people there, Kim knew that to pursue her dreams, she needed to move beyond Columbus. She needed to be in a place where opportunities in fashion were more abundant. After graduating from Columbus High School in 1988, she made the bold decision to move to Atlanta. At the time, Atlanta was growing as a cultural hub in the South, and while it wasn't New York or Los Angeles, it was a city where young talents could start making connections and begin building their careers. For Kim, it was the first step in her journey toward becoming a model.

Moving to Atlanta was a major decision, but Kim was determined to succeed. It wasn't easy leaving the comfort of her hometown and stepping into a new environment where she knew fewer people. Yet, her drive was unmatched. She took on different jobs and assignments to make ends meet, but she never lost focus on her goal of breaking into the fashion world. Kim knew that this part of her journey would be challenging, but she embraced the hustle and the uncertainty because she believed in her vision.

In Atlanta, Kim began to build her network. She sought out opportunities to be seen, attending events, and meeting people in the industry. She also began working on her portfolio. Modelling isn't just about taking photos; it's about learning how to move, how to pose, and how to tell a story through a lens. Kim took this part of her development seriously, working with photographers to create a body of work that showcased her unique style and ability. Every photoshoot was a learning experience, and Kim was committed to growing and perfecting her craft.

Atlanta became a stepping stone for Kim. While the city offered opportunities, it also prepared her for the larger fashion capitals she would later encounter. Kim wasn't just honing her skills as a model; she was also learning the business of fashion. She understood that success in this industry required more than just a pretty face; it demanded professionalism, patience, and the ability to navigate the ups and downs of a competitive field. These early years in Atlanta built the foundation for her later success.

One of the most significant moments in Kim's early career came when she caught the attention of agents and talent scouts. While she was building her portfolio in Atlanta, word started to spread about the new, up-and-coming model with a captivating presence. Kim's confidence, combined with her natural beauty and determination, made her stand out. It wasn't long before she received an offer that would change the trajectory of her career: the opportunity to move to New York City and take her modelling to the next level.

For Kim, this was the moment she had been waiting for. New York City was the heart of the fashion world in the United States, and if she wanted to truly make a name for herself, it was the place she needed to be. Moving to New York represented the next step in her journey, but it also came with new challenges and risks. Leaving Atlanta wasn't easy, especially as she had started to find a rhythm in her work there. Yet, Kim knew that real growth came from stepping outside of her comfort zone, and New York offered the chance to do just that.

Before making the move, Kim reflected on her journey so far. The girl from Columbus, Georgia, who had always dreamed of becoming a model, was now on the cusp of something great. Atlanta had given her the opportunity to learn, grow, and start building her career. The connections she made, the experiences she had, and the lessons she learned in Atlanta would be the stepping stones she would carry with her as she took her talents to New York.

Kim's time in Atlanta wasn't just about modelling. It was about finding herself, understanding the industry, and preparing for the challenges ahead. The decision to leave her hometown and start over in a new city wasn't easy, but it shaped her into the determined and resilient woman she would become. Every step of the way, Kim trusted her instincts, worked hard, and never gave up on her dream of one day seeing her name in lights.

Her move to New York marked the beginning of the next chapter in her life. Atlanta had served its purpose as a launchpad, and now Kim was ready to soar.

# CHAPTER 2

# Starting in the Modelling World

**M**oving to New York was a huge step for Kim Porter. It marked the beginning of her modelling career and, ultimately, the foundation of the life she was destined to build. Coming from Columbus, Georgia, Kim had always dreamed big. New York was the city where dreams were made, but for her, it was also a city full of challenges, competition, and the unknown.

When Kim arrived in New York, she faced a new reality. Modelling was one of the most competitive industries, and for a young Black woman in the 1990s, the hurdles were even greater. But Kim was determined. She wasn't just another pretty face hoping to make it. She was ready to put in the work, take risks, and create a lasting impact.

## Early Struggles and Determination

At the beginning, it wasn't easy. Kim had to hustle just like many other aspiring models. Her days were filled with auditions, meetings with casting directors, and long waits in line with hundreds of other girls. She had no guarantee of success. Rejection was a constant reality, but instead of letting it bring her down, she used it as motivation.

Kim's resilience during those early days in New York was a testament to her character. She knew that breaking into the modelling world would require more than just her looks. She needed the right connections, strong networking skills, and the ability to stand out in a sea of talented individuals. Still, she never let the competition shake her confidence.

One of the toughest challenges Kim faced was the limited representation of Black women in mainstream fashion. At the time, the fashion industry was predominantly focused on a certain "look," often favouring lighter-skinned or European features. Kim knew that this made her journey harder, but it also gave her a deeper sense of purpose. She wanted to change the industry and show that beauty came in all forms.

**Her First Big Break**

Kim's persistence paid off when she got her first big break. After months of hard work and auditions, she was finally noticed by casting agents who saw something special in her. Her natural grace, stunning beauty, and captivating presence made her stand out. She landed her first major job—a fashion spread in one of the top magazines of the time.

That moment was life-changing for Kim. It was the validation she needed to know that she was on the right path. It wasn't just about landing one job; it was the beginning of something much bigger. As her reputation grew, more opportunities started to open. She began working with some of the biggest names in the industry, including top fashion photographers and designers.

This turning point in her career proved that her hard work had been worth it. Kim was no longer just another aspiring model—she was a force to be reckoned with. Her name started gaining recognition, and soon, she found herself on the radar of industry insiders.

## Navigating the Industry

Even as her career started to take off, the modelling industry presented many challenges. The competition was still fierce, and maintaining a steady stream of work wasn't guaranteed. But Kim wasn't one to rest on her laurels. She knew that consistency was key, and she kept pushing forward, always looking for the next opportunity.

One of the most important things she learned was how to navigate the complex relationships in the fashion world. Networking became essential, and Kim quickly understood the value of building strong connections with the right people. She attended industry events, met with photographers, and developed relationships with designers. These connections helped her land more jobs and solidified her place in the modelling scene.

Kim also understood the importance of versatility. In a world where trends changed quickly, being adaptable was crucial. She worked hard to ensure she could deliver different looks and styles depending on what was needed. Whether it was a high-fashion editorial shoot or a commercial campaign, Kim knew how to adjust, and that made her stand out even more.

## Breaking Barriers as a Black Woman in Fashion

As a Black woman in the industry, Kim faced certain challenges that many of her peers didn't. At that time, Black models were often underrepresented on magazine covers, in ad campaigns, and on runways. Despite this, Kim's success helped break some of those barriers. She became one of the few models who was regularly booked for high-profile jobs, proving that diversity in beauty was not just possible but also powerful.

Kim understood that she was not only building her own career but also paving the way for others. Her presence in major campaigns and fashion shows sent a message to the industry: Black beauty deserved recognition. She embraced this role with pride, knowing that she was helping to shift perceptions within an industry that had been slow to change.

## Working with Top Brands and Photographers

One of the highlights of Kim's career in New York was the opportunity to work with some of the most influential names in fashion. She posed for well-known photographers who had worked with the top supermodels of the time. Their photoshoots helped boost her visibility and made her a recognizable face in the industry.

As she gained more exposure, Kim started to work with international fashion brands. These campaigns not only expanded her portfolio but also showcased her ability to adapt to different fashion styles, from editorial to commercial. Her growing success in New York meant that she was becoming a sought-after model, and soon her face could be seen in advertisements and magazines across the country.

## A Model with Purpose

Even as her career grew, Kim never forgot why she had started. Modelling was more than just a career for her—it was a platform. She wanted to use her success to inspire other women, especially young Black women, to chase their dreams and not be afraid of the challenges that stood in their way.

Her time in New York was not only about building a successful career but also about making a difference. She believed that beauty was diverse and that the fashion world needed to reflect that diversity. Through her work, Kim Porter helped open doors for future generations of Black models, leaving a legacy in the industry.

Kim Porter's time in New York was just the beginning of her journey in the modelling world. While it was filled with challenges, rejections, and hard-earned successes, it laid the foundation for the remarkable career that would follow. Her ability to persevere in a tough industry, her determination to break barriers, and her unwavering belief in her own potential made her a force to be reckoned with.

# Key Modelling Gigs and Magazine Appearances

Kim Porter's journey in the modelling world began when she moved to New York, a bold step that allowed her to break into a highly competitive industry. With her stunning looks, poise, and unique presence, she quickly gained recognition. She worked with several major brands and appeared on prominent magazine covers, which not only solidified her status in the industry but also helped to open doors for future opportunities.

One of Kim's early breakthroughs was landing a photoshoot with **Essence**, a magazine known for celebrating Black beauty, culture, and empowerment. Appearing on **Essence** was a significant milestone for Kim, as it allowed her to reach a wider audience while representing Black women in an industry that often-lacked diversity. The exposure she received from **Essence** positioned her as a role model for young Black women who were aspiring to enter fashion and entertainment.

Another notable appearance came when Kim was featured in **Runway** magazine. This opportunity highlighted her versatility as a model, demonstrating her ability to transition between high fashion and commercial projects. Kim's work with **Runway** not only elevated her career but also showed her adaptability in various settings, whether it was a high-end runway shoot or a more commercial, consumer-driven project.

Throughout her career, Kim collaborated with several top photographers who helped shape her public image. Working with renowned photographers like **Patrick Demarchelier** and **Bruce Weber**, Kim's portfolio grew, showcasing her ability to embody various styles and aesthetics. These collaborations also allowed her to gain respect in the fashion community as someone who could hold her own alongside other top models.

One of the most memorable parts of Kim's modelling career was her ability to work with fashion brands that were inclusive of diverse models. For example, her work with **Sean John**, the clothing line launched by her long-time partner Sean "Diddy" Combs, gave her a platform that merged both her professional and personal life. The campaigns she participated in not only highlighted her beauty but also celebrated her as a key figure in Diddy's life. Being involved in Sean John's marketing helped boost both the brand and her own visibility, making her a prominent figure in fashion.

Despite her modelling work often being behind the scenes compared to other high-profile models, Kim was a recognized face in the industry. She graced smaller; niche fashion magazines that catered to a growing audience interested in diverse representations of beauty. This allowed her to build a steady career without needing to constantly be in the public spotlight, which aligned with her personality.

# The Challenges of Being a Black Woman in the Fashion Industry

As Kim navigated the fashion world, she faced many challenges that were common for Black women in the industry, especially in the 1990s and early 2000s. During this time, diversity was not a priority for many fashion houses or magazines. Kim, like many of her peers, often encountered systemic racism and biases that made it more difficult for her to secure high-profile gigs compared to her white counterparts.

One of the biggest challenges Kim faced was the lack of representation in major fashion campaigns. At the time, the fashion industry heavily favored Eurocentric beauty standards, and Black models were often overlooked for prestigious opportunities. This meant that, despite her talent and beauty, Kim had to work twice as hard to be noticed in an industry that was slow to embrace diversity. Many top designers and brands chose to work with a very narrow range of models, making it difficult for Kim and others to break into mainstream fashion circles.

Another issue Kim faced was the typecasting that was prevalent in the modelling world. Black models were often pigeonholed into specific roles or types of campaigns. For example, they were frequently cast in urban or streetwear campaigns, while being overlooked for luxury or high-fashion opportunities. While Kim embraced the work she did with brands like Sean John, she likely would have been offered fewer opportunities in high-fashion settings simply because of her race. This type of typecasting limited her range of opportunities and made it harder to showcase her full talent.

Colourism also played a significant role in the challenges Kim faced. Even within the Black modelling community, lighter-skinned models were often favored over those with darker skin. This bias further reduced the number of opportunities available to Black models who didn't fit the industry's narrow standard of beauty. Kim's own experience in this environment, while successful, would have undoubtedly been shaped by these pressures and biases, as she navigated an industry that often failed to celebrate a wide spectrum of Black beauty.

Despite these challenges, Kim's resilience helped her carve out a space in the industry where she could thrive. She was strategic in the types of work she pursued, aligning herself with brands that valued diversity and wanted to promote Black culture. This is evident in her work with **Essence** magazine, a publication that was built on showcasing Black excellence and beauty. By partnering with these types of platforms, Kim not only advanced her own career but also contributed to the slow yet steady push for more diversity in the fashion industry.

In addition to the external pressures of racism and colourism, Kim also had to deal with the everyday stresses of being a Black woman in an industry that is notorious for its superficiality. The pressure to maintain a specific look and constantly conform to the industry's beauty standards would have been immense.

This can often lead to mental and emotional fatigue, especially for models of colour who face additional scrutiny about their appearance, hair, and even body type.

However, Kim's influence went beyond her individual experiences. She served as an inspiration for the next generation of Black models, many of whom entered the industry at a time when it was more open to diversity, thanks to the groundwork laid by women like Kim. Her success and presence in the modelling world showed that, despite the challenges, it was possible for Black women to make their mark in an industry that often tried to keep them out. Kim's legacy continues to inspire young Black models today, many of whom see her as a trailblazer who helped create space for them in a competitive and often exclusive industry.

Ultimately, while Kim Porter's modelling career was filled with incredible achievements, it was also shaped by the realities of being a Black woman in a predominantly white industry. Her perseverance, grace, and strength allowed her to rise above the barriers placed before her and leave a legacy in the worlds of fashion and beauty.

# CHAPTER 3

# Love and Family

Kim Porter's relationships with Al B. Sure! and Sean "Diddy" Combs were significant parts of her life, shaping not only her personal journey but also playing an important role in her public image. Each relationship brought different experiences, joys, and challenges, and through it all, Kim maintained grace and love for her children, ensuring they were always her priority.

In the late 1980s, Kim began dating the popular R&B singer Al B. Sure! Born Albert Joseph Brown III, Al B. Sure! was a well-known figure in the music world at the time, with hits like "Nite and Day" that made him a household name. Kim, who was then working to establish her career in modelling, met Al B. Sure! when they were both rising stars. Their relationship soon blossomed into a meaningful connection, leading to the birth of their son, Quincy Brown, in 1991.

For Kim, becoming a mother for the first time was a life-changing experience. She often spoke about how motherhood gave her a new sense of purpose. While her relationship with Al B. Sure! didn't last, the bond they shared through Quincy remained strong. Kim was always determined to provide Quincy with the best upbringing possible, despite the challenges that came with co-parenting.

Quincy was named after legendary music producer Quincy Jones, reflecting the musical influence in their lives. Kim ensured that Quincy had a stable, loving environment even as she navigated the complexities of her relationship with Al B. Sure! She wanted her son to grow up feeling loved by both parents, and though their romantic relationship ended, Kim and Al B. Sure! remained connected as co-parents. Their shared focus on Quincy's well-being was a priority for both, and Quincy's relationship with his father continued to be strong.

Kim Porter's most well-known relationship was with Sean "Diddy" Combs, one of the most influential figures in the music industry. Kim met Diddy in the early 1990s, when he was still making his way in the business. At the time, Diddy, born Sean Combs, was a budding music producer who was on the cusp of becoming one of the biggest names in hip-hop.

Their relationship started as a friendship, with both being part of the same social circles in New York. Kim, with her modelling background and connection to the fashion world, and Diddy, with his growing presence in the music industry, complemented each other. They shared similar aspirations, work ethics, and values, which made their connection even stronger.

As their friendship grew into a romantic relationship, they became one of the most high-profile couples in the entertainment world. The media often followed their every move, and their relationship became the subject of public fascination. Despite the attention,

Kim was always focused on creating a strong family environment.

In 1998, Kim and Diddy welcomed their first child together, Christian Combs. Kim embraced motherhood once again, this time raising her son during the ever-growing fame and success that surrounded Diddy. As Diddy's career skyrocketed, Kim remained his constant supporter, balancing her personal life with the pressures of being in the spotlight. She was often described as Diddy's "rock" during the early years of his career, providing him with emotional support while raising their children.

Kim and Diddy's relationship had its share of ups and downs, like many long-term relationships. While they shared a deep connection and built a family together, the pressures of fame and the complexities of their individual careers sometimes caused tension. Their relationship was on-and-off for several years, with multiple breakups and reconciliations along the way.

Throughout it all, Kim remained a steady and loving presence in Diddy's life. Even during their breakups, they often remained close, with both prioritizing their children above all else. Kim's ability to maintain grace and poise during public breakups was admired by many, as she navigated a very public relationship with a level of maturity and dignity that was rare in the entertainment world.

In 2006, Kim and Diddy welcomed twin daughters, D'Lila Star and Jessie James. The birth of the twins brought a new sense of joy to their lives, and Kim's focus once again turned to raising her children in a supportive and loving environment. As a mother of four, she worked hard to ensure that her children were well-rounded and grounded, despite their parents' fame.

Kim and Diddy's relationship came to an official end in 2007, but even after their romantic ties were severed, they remained extremely close. Their bond as co-parents was strong, and they often spent time together as a family, attending events and celebrating holidays. Kim and Diddy were committed to raising their children with love, stability, and a sense of unity, regardless of their romantic relationship status.

What made Kim and Diddy's relationship unique was the strong bond they maintained even after their breakup. Many close to the couple remarked on the deep respect and love they had for each other, even as they navigated their lives separately. Diddy often referred to Kim as his best friend, and their connection went beyond romance—it was built on trust, understanding, and a shared commitment to their children.

Diddy has spoken publicly about how much Kim meant to him, calling her his soulmate even after their relationship ended. He often shared how Kim's influence made him a better man and father. Their friendship became an example of how two people can maintain love and respect for one another, even if their romantic relationship didn't last.

When Kim passed away in 2018, Diddy was devastated. He paid tribute to her in several heartfelt public statements, sharing how deeply he loved and admired her. He called her his "guiding light" and expressed how much she meant to him and their family. Her death left a profound impact on Diddy and their children, but it also highlighted the lasting love and bond they shared.

Kim Porter's relationships with Al B. Sure! and Diddy were central to her life, but her true legacy lies in the love and care she gave to her children. Despite the fame and public attention, she was a devoted mother who made her children her top priority. Both Al B. Sure! and Diddy have expressed their gratitude for the way Kim raised their children, and her influence continues to live on through them.

Her relationships, while filled with public attention, were deeply rooted in love, respect, and family. Kim's ability to maintain grace and strength throughout the ups and downs of her relationships is part of what made her such a beloved figure. She showed that love is not always simple, but with dedication and care, it can create a legacy.

# Becoming a mother to Quincy, Christian, and the Twins

Motherhood played a central role in Kim Porter's life. For her, being a mother was not just a responsibility but a source of immense joy and purpose. Each of her children—Quincy, Christian, and her twin daughters D'Lila Star and Jessie James—brought a new chapter of love, growth, and learning into her life. She cherished the opportunity to raise them and took pride in her role as a mother, prioritizing her children's well-being over everything else.

Her journey as a mother began with the birth of her first son, Quincy Brown, in 1991. Quincy was born from her relationship with R&B singer Al B. Sure! Although her relationship with Quincy's father didn't last, Kim made sure that her son grew up in a supportive and nurturing environment. She worked hard to maintain a sense of normalcy in Quincy's life, despite the challenges of navigating the public eye. Quincy's bond with his mother was strong, and even as he grew older and pursued his own career in acting and music, he remained deeply connected to Kim.

When Kim later entered a relationship with music mogul Sean "Diddy" Combs, her family expanded with the birth of their first son, Christian Combs, in 1998. Christian's arrival brought a new wave of joy into Kim's life. She embraced the challenges of raising two boys and balanced her growing family with her career in modelling and entrepreneurship. As a mother to Christian, Kim worked to instil values of humility, respect, and hard work. She made sure her children understood the importance of staying grounded, even though they were surrounded by wealth and fame.

In 2006, Kim gave birth to twin daughters, D'Lila Star and Jessie James. The arrival of her daughters was a special moment for Kim, marking the expansion of her family in a significant way. Raising twins brought new challenges, but Kim embraced motherhood with the same grace and strength she had always shown. She often described her daughters as the "light of her life" and devoted herself to giving them a loving, supportive upbringing.

For Kim, motherhood wasn't just about providing material things or a comfortable life for her children. It was about being present, offering guidance, and showing unconditional love. She was known for spending quality time with her kids, whether it was at home, on vacations, or during their public appearances together. Her bond with her children was strong, and she made sure to nurture each of them individually, understanding their unique personalities and needs. Even as her children began to step into the public spotlight, Kim remained their anchor, offering love and support at every turn.

Her role as a mother was a defining part of her identity. She wanted her children to grow up with the values she held dear—kindness, empathy, and a sense of purpose. Despite her own fame and success, Kim was determined to give her children as normal a life as possible. Her home was a place of love and stability, and she worked hard to shield her children from the pressures that often come with growing up in the public eye.

Kim's bond with each of her children was strong, and they often expressed their love and gratitude for her. Quincy has spoken about how his mother was his rock, someone who always supported him no matter what. Christian, who has pursued a career in music, often reflects on how his mother's love and guidance helped shape him into the person he is today. For the twins, Kim's nurturing presence was always there, and she made sure that they felt loved and protected.

# Co-Parenting with Diddy and Their Strong Bond

Kim Porter and Sean "Diddy" Combs had a long and complex relationship, filled with highs and lows. While they eventually ended their romantic relationship in 2007, they remained committed to raising their children together and maintained a close bond as co-parents. Their dedication to their children's well-being was the foundation of their relationship, and they both worked hard to provide a loving and supportive environment for Quincy, Christian, and the twins.

Co-parenting wasn't always easy, especially given the public nature of their relationship. Yet, Kim and Diddy managed to navigate their differences with grace and respect. They prioritized their children above all else, ensuring that the kids always felt loved and supported, even when their parents were no longer romantically involved. Their ability to co-parent effectively was a testament to the deep respect and love they had for each other, despite the challenges that came with their breakups.

One of the key aspects of their co-parenting relationship was communication. Kim and Diddy understood that in order to raise their children well, they had to maintain open lines of communication. They made decisions together, consulted each other on important matters, and worked hard to be present for their kids during important milestones. Whether it was attending school events, birthday parties, or public appearances, both Kim and Diddy were there, showing their children that they were a united front when it came to parenting.

Their co-parenting relationship was also rooted in mutual respect. Despite the end of their romantic relationship, Kim and Diddy always spoke highly of each other in public. They never allowed their personal differences to interfere with their shared goal of raising happy, well-adjusted children. Diddy often praised Kim for being a wonderful mother, and she, in turn, expressed her admiration for his dedication to their family. This mutual respect helped create a harmonious environment for their children to grow up in.

Over the years, Diddy has shared how much he valued Kim's presence in his life, not just as the mother of his children but as his best friend. Even after their split, Kim remained a constant figure in Diddy's life, offering him advice and support. Their bond was more than just co-parenting; they shared a deep friendship that allowed them to work together in raising their family. Kim's passing in 2018 left a void in Diddy's life, and he has spoken openly about how much he misses her and how their bond as co-parents was one of the most important relationships he ever had.

For their children, seeing their parents work together as a team, despite their romantic separation, was a powerful example of love and partnership. Kim and Diddy's ability to co-parent with such grace and dedication left a lasting impact on their children. It showed them the importance of family, communication, and respect, and these values continue to guide Quincy, Christian, D'Lila Star, and Jessie James as they grow older.

In the years since Kim's passing, Diddy has made it clear that her legacy as a mother will always be honored. He has continued to support and celebrate their children, keeping Kim's memory alive in their lives. The bond that Kim and Diddy shared as co-parents is a testament to the power of love, even in the face of life's challenges.

# CHAPTER 4

# Motherhood at the Heart

K im Porter's life was undeniably shaped by her deep love for her four children: Quincy, Christian, and the twin girls, D'Lila Star and Jessie James. Although her career in the entertainment industry brought her fame, it was her role as a mother that she cherished the most. Her devotion to her children defined her life, and she was dedicated to ensuring they grew up in a loving, balanced environment, despite the pressures of celebrity life.

From the start, Kim embraced motherhood with an open heart. Her first child, Quincy, was born during her relationship with singer Al B. Sure! Even though their romantic relationship ended, Kim made sure that Quincy had a strong connection with both his biological father and Sean "Diddy" Combs, whom she began dating shortly after Quincy's birth. When Quincy was adopted by Diddy, the bond between them only strengthened. Kim was able to foster a unique family dynamic where Quincy was raised with love from both of his fathers. This nurturing environment helped Quincy develop into the well-rounded, successful young man he is today.

When Christian Combs was born, Kim's role as a mother deepened. She had always wanted a family, and Christian's arrival fulfilled part of that dream. Raising two boys in the public eye was not an easy task, but Kim was committed to protecting their childhoods from the chaos that often comes with fame. She believed in teaching her children values like kindness, respect, and responsibility. These were qualities she instilled in them from a young age, making sure they understood that the family's wealth and status didn't mean they could live without purpose.

One of Kim's key principles in raising her children was balance. While she enjoyed the privileges of a glamorous life, she was equally devoted to creating a stable home environment. Kim was determined to provide her children with a sense of normalcy, even though their father, Diddy, was one of the biggest names in the music industry. She ensured that their home life was filled with love, warmth, and structure. Her children were encouraged to express themselves freely, but they were also taught discipline and the importance of hard work.

In 2006, Kim welcomed twin daughters, D'Lila Star and Jessie James. The arrival of the twins brought immense joy to Kim, and she fully embraced her new role as the mother of two girls. Kim's approach to raising the twins mirrored the same principles she had applied to her sons. She believed in nurturing each child's individuality while fostering a close bond between them. Even though the girls were identical twins, Kim made sure to celebrate their unique personalities, helping them develop into confident, independent young women.

Family was at the center of everything Kim did. Whether it was planning birthday parties, attending school events, or taking family vacations, Kim was always present for her children. She valued quality time with her family and was known for hosting intimate gatherings at home. These events were an opportunity for the children to enjoy time with both parents and extended family. Despite her busy schedule, Kim made sure that her children knew they were her priority.

Her dedication to her children didn't stop with their physical well-being. Kim was deeply committed to their emotional development as well. She believed that raising emotionally intelligent children was just as important as ensuring their physical health. This involved creating a space where her children could openly express their feelings, whether it was about their personal lives or their experience growing up with famous parents. Kim was always available to listen and offer guidance, and her children often describe her as the one person they could always turn to for support.

The foundation that Kim built for her children also extended to their spiritual growth. While she didn't publicly discuss her personal faith often, those close to her knew that Kim was a woman of strong spiritual beliefs. She raised her children with an understanding of the importance of faith, teaching them to stay grounded and to appreciate life's blessings. This spiritual grounding helped her children navigate the complexities of growing up in the public eye.

As a mother, Kim balanced providing her children with every opportunity while ensuring they understood the value of hard work and perseverance. She didn't want her children to rely solely on the family's status; instead, she encouraged them to find their own paths in life. Quincy, Christian, and the twins have all pursued their own careers and passions, and they often credit their mother for instilling in them the drive to succeed. Christian followed in his father's footsteps, pursuing a career in music, while Quincy found success as an actor. The twins, though still young, are already showing signs of inheriting their mother's poise and confidence.

Kim's legacy as a mother is reflected in the bond her children share with each other and with their father, Diddy. Even after Kim and Diddy ended their romantic relationship, they remained committed co-parents, ensuring that their children never felt divided between them. They often came together for important family events, birthdays, and holidays, providing a united front for their children. This sense of unity was essential for the emotional well-being of the children, and it's something that Diddy has publicly acknowledged many times.

Kim's influence on her children extends beyond their childhood years. In many ways, she prepared them for life's challenges by giving them the tools to be strong, independent, and kind-hearted individuals. The values she instilled in them—humility, hard work, love for family, and faith—are qualities they continue to carry with them today.

In the aftermath of Kim's passing, her children have spoken openly about the profound impact she had on their lives. Quincy, Christian, D'Lila, and Jessie often post heartfelt tributes to their mother on social media, reflecting on the lessons she taught them and the love she gave so freely. Her legacy as a mother is one of unconditional love, support, and an unshakeable commitment to raising her children to be the best versions of themselves.

# Balancing Her Career and Family Life

Kim Porter was a woman who wore many hats throughout her life. She was a successful model, an actress, an entrepreneur, and, most importantly, a devoted mother. While her public life was often in the spotlight due to her high-profile relationships and career in the entertainment industry, her true pride and joy were her children. One of Kim's greatest challenges was finding the delicate balance between pursuing her professional goals and being fully present in her children's lives.

The entertainment industry is known for its fast pace, demanding schedules, and high levels of pressure, making it difficult to juggle personal and professional responsibilities. For Kim, managing this challenge was a top priority. Despite the demands of her career, she consistently prioritized her children, ensuring that they received the care and attention they needed. Friends and family often praised her for how seamlessly she managed to move between the runway or set and home life.

One way Kim achieved this balance was by setting clear boundaries. When she was working, she was fully committed to her projects. But when she was home with her children, she made it a point to focus on them without distractions. This ability to be present in both spaces allowed her to thrive in both roles. Her modelling and acting work was something she loved, but she always kept family at the center of her life.

As a mother of four, her responsibilities extended far beyond her career. Her children—Quincy, Christian, and her twins, D'Lila Star and Jessie James—were her motivation. She made sure to create a sense of stability for them, despite the public nature of their family life. Kim was careful to ensure her children grew up grounded, even while they were surrounded by the glitz and glamor of the entertainment world. She kept their routines structured, made sure they had normal childhood experiences, and shielded them from much of the pressure that often comes with being in the public eye.

A key part of balancing her career and family life was the support system she built around her. Kim maintained close relationships with her family and friends, who helped her manage her hectic schedule. This network of trusted individuals enabled her to confidently pursue her professional goals, knowing her children were always well cared for. It was this sense of community that gave Kim the peace of mind needed to succeed in both realms.

Diddy, the father of three of her children, was a significant part of this support system. Even after their romantic relationship ended, Kim and Diddy maintained a strong co-parenting relationship, working together to ensure their children had a stable upbringing. Their ability to co-parent effectively was a reflection of Kim's maturity and dedication to her family. They remained partners in raising their children, celebrating milestones together, and providing a united front for their kids.

Another strategy Kim used to balance her career and family life was including her children in her world whenever possible. For example, her son Quincy followed in her footsteps and pursued a career in entertainment, allowing her to offer guidance and support in a meaningful way. She encouraged her children to explore their interests, whether in music, fashion, or acting, and was always there to offer advice based on her own experiences. This connection between her personal and professional life allowed her to maintain a close bond with her children while continuing to work.

Kim was also mindful of the importance of self-care, both for herself and her children. She understood that in order to be fully present in their lives, she needed to take care of her own well-being. Whether it was taking time to focus on her health, wellness, or simply stepping away from the limelight to recharge, Kim made sure to practice balance in every aspect of her life.

One of the most admirable things about Kim was that, despite her success, she never let it overshadow her role as a mother. She taught her children the importance of humility, kindness, and staying grounded. She made it clear to them that fame and success should not define their worth or character. By focusing on these values, Kim ensured that her children grew up with a strong sense of self, which was key to them navigating their own paths in life.

## Lessons She Passed on to Her Children

Kim Porter believed in raising her children with strong values, and the lessons she imparted to them have become central to how they carry themselves today. One of the core lessons she taught her children was the importance of family. She made sure they understood that no matter what successes or challenges they faced, family would always be their foundation. This sense of loyalty and commitment to one another helped her children develop close relationships with each other and the rest of their family.

Another lesson Kim instilled in her children was the value of hard work. Having achieved success in her own right, Kim knew the importance of perseverance and dedication. She encouraged her children to pursue their dreams with the same level of passion and determination that she had. Whether it was Quincy's journey into acting and music or Christian's venture into modelling, Kim made sure her children knew that nothing worth having comes without effort. This message of hard work resonated with them, pushing them to carve out their own paths while remaining true to themselves.

Kim also emphasized the importance of self-respect and kindness. She raised her children to treat everyone with dignity and compassion, no matter their background or status. In a world where they were constantly surrounded by wealth and fame, Kim ensured that her children stayed humble and empathetic. She believed that true success was not measured by material achievements but by how one treats others.

In addition, Kim taught her children the power of resilience. Life in the public eye comes with its share of challenges, and Kim wanted her children to be prepared to handle adversity with grace and strength. She led by example, showing them how to remain calm and focused in difficult times. Whether dealing with personal struggles or the pressures of fame, Kim's calm demeanour and positive outlook helped her children navigate their own challenges.

Lastly, Kim passed on the importance of gratitude. Despite the privileges her children enjoyed, she made sure they never took anything for granted. She encouraged them to be thankful for their blessings and to give back whenever they could. Kim believed that living a life of service and gratitude was key to true happiness, and this lesson has stayed with her children as they continue to grow and succeed in their own lives.

# CHAPTER 5

# Behind the Music

K im Porter's influence on Sean "Diddy" Combs and his career is often understated, yet it was an essential part of the larger picture of his success in the music industry. While Diddy is widely recognized as a powerhouse producer, rapper, and business mogul, Kim stood beside him as a steady, supportive force during some of the most pivotal moments in his career. Her presence wasn't just about being a partner in his personal life; she also had a quiet but profound impact on his professional journey.

Kim and Diddy met in the early 1990s, during a time when Diddy was rapidly building his empire at Bad Boy Records. Their connection was instant, and although they had an on-and-off relationship, Kim's influence never wavered, both as the mother of his children and as someone who played a behind-the-scenes role in shaping his career. She understood the world Diddy operated in—the late-night studio sessions, the pressures of managing artists, and the demands of running a record label. Instead of just being a bystander, Kim was involved in ways that demonstrated her understanding of the industry.

One of Kim's key roles in Diddy's life was providing emotional stability. The music industry can be brutal, with intense competition and the constant pressure to produce hits. Diddy faced numerous challenges, from legal battles to the emotional toll of losing close friends like the Notorious B.I.G. Through these ups and downs, Kim remained a constant presence in his life. She had a way of grounding him, reminding him of what truly mattered: family, loyalty, and integrity. Her ability to be both a partner and a confidante allowed Diddy to focus on his work without losing sight of his personal values.

During the early stages of Diddy's career, especially during the peak years of Bad Boy Records, Kim was often seen at his side at major industry events, but her involvement went far deeper than public appearances. She offered advice on business matters, even if her suggestions were informal. Diddy has often spoken about how Kim had a strong sense of people, and she would help him discern who to trust and who to keep at arm's length. In an industry where relationships can make or break careers, Kim's instinct for people became invaluable to Diddy as he navigated the complexities of running a record label.

The emotional support Kim provided was equally critical. One of the most challenging moments in Diddy's life was the tragic death of the Notorious B.I.G. in 1997. The loss of his close friend and label's biggest star sent shockwaves through Bad Boy Records. During this time, Kim's presence was a pillar of strength for Diddy. She helped him process his grief while also encouraging him to channel his pain into his music. It was around this time that Diddy released the tribute song "I'll Be Missing You," which became a global hit. While Diddy received widespread recognition for the song, Kim's emotional support during that dark period helped him stay focused on his work when the loss could have easily derailed his career.

Kim's role in Diddy's life wasn't just about emotional support. She was also instrumental in helping him maintain a balanced personal life, despite the chaos that often surrounded them. With Diddy's career taking off, the demands on his time were relentless. From running a record label to launching clothing lines and acting ventures, Diddy's life was always moving at full speed. Kim played a crucial role in making sure there was harmony between his work and family life. She took care of their children, providing a stable home life that allowed Diddy to focus on his career without neglecting his responsibilities as a father.

Kim's role as a mother also intertwined with Diddy's career. Christian Combs, their son, has followed in his father's footsteps, pursuing a career in music and fashion. Kim was always supportive of Christian's ambitions, and she played an important role in shaping his early career. Her guidance, combined with Diddy's influence, helped Christian navigate the pressures of growing up in the public eye and entering the same industry that made his father a star. Kim's nurturing spirit allowed Christian to develop his talents while also maintaining a sense of humility, something that both Diddy and Kim valued deeply.

While Kim preferred to remain out of the direct spotlight, her influence on Diddy's brand extended to the way he presented himself. She had an eye for fashion and understood the importance of image in the entertainment world. Whether it was selecting outfits for major appearances or helping Diddy with the visual direction of his music videos, Kim's input helped elevate his brand. Her taste in fashion was refined yet accessible, and she knew how to blend the high glamour of the music industry with a sense of authenticity. This balance was something Diddy valued as he built his image as a multifaceted entrepreneur.

Kim also had a unique role as a sounding board for Diddy's creative ideas. While she wasn't a musician herself, she had a deep appreciation for the arts and a natural understanding of what worked. Diddy often sought her opinions on everything from new music to branding decisions. She was one of the few people in his inner circle who could give him honest feedback, and Diddy trusted her judgment implicitly. Her ability to see things from a different perspective allowed her to offer insights that others might miss, making her an invaluable part of Diddy's creative process.

As Diddy's career evolved, with ventures in fashion, television, and spirits, Kim's role remained consistent. She was never just a passive participant in his world; she was an active force who contributed to his success in quiet but significant ways. Whether it was offering support during tough times, helping him maintain a balance between work and family, or simply being someone, he could rely on for honesty, Kim's presence in Diddy's life was essential to his career longevity.

In the years following Kim's passing, Diddy has spoken publicly about how much she meant to him, not just as the mother of his children but as a vital part of his journey. Her influence continues to resonate, both in his personal life and in his career. While the public may remember Kim Porter for her beauty and grace, those who knew her best understood the depth of her contributions to Diddy's success and the music industry.

Kim Porter's role in Diddy's career and the music world was one of quiet strength and unwavering support. She played a key part in shaping his career, offering emotional, personal, and even creative guidance. While she may have stayed out of the limelight, her influence was deeply felt, and her legacy continues to live on through Diddy's work and their children.

## Her Influence Behind the Scenes

Kim Porter may have been best known for her modelling and high-profile relationship with Sean "Diddy" Combs, but her impact behind the scenes was far more substantial than many realized. Her presence was deeply felt in the music industry and among her closest circles, where she quietly influenced decisions, helped foster creativity, and acted as a stabilizing force for many.

Her role in Diddy's life went beyond being the mother of his children. She became a sounding board for his ideas and often gave feedback on projects. Those close to them knew that Kim was a trusted confidante, someone Diddy turned to when making important decisions. This kind of trust shows just how valuable Kim was to the creative process, even when she wasn't directly in the spotlight. She understood the industry well, not just as an observer but as someone who experienced it firsthand through her connections and relationships.

Kim had an incredible ability to maintain calm in a world that often moved at a fast and chaotic pace. She kept her circle grounded, offering advice that went beyond business and extended to personal life. This ability to balance both aspects of her life is what made her so influential. Those who worked closely with Diddy and other artists often noted that Kim brought a sense of stability. While others were caught up in the pressures and excitement of the entertainment industry, she remained focused on what truly mattered: creating meaningful work and supporting the people she loved.

Kim was also known for her discretion. In an industry where gossip and leaks were common, she was someone who could be trusted to keep personal and professional matters private. Her loyalty helped her maintain long-lasting relationships with key figures in the industry. She provided a safe space for artists to express themselves, knowing they could count on her discretion. This trust earned her deep respect from those around her and positioned her as someone people could confide in, both creatively and personally.

# Supporting Artists and the Creative Process

Kim Porter wasn't just a passive observer in the music industry; she actively supported the creative process for many artists, both established and upcoming. Her influence was especially significant in the career of Diddy. Being one of the most influential figures in the music industry, Diddy often relied on Kim for her opinions, feedback, and insights. She helped him stay grounded while he built a music empire, guiding him in both personal and business matters. Her contributions were not just emotional support but also practical input that helped shape decisions on songs, collaborations, and creative directions.

Kim had a deep understanding of music and the people behind it. Her keen intuition allowed her to understand what worked and what didn't, not just from a business perspective, but from an artistic point of view. When Diddy or other artists were working on projects, she was often consulted for her thoughts. She could offer constructive criticism, but in a way that was uplifting and supportive. Her words motivated those around her to do better without making them feel torn down. This rare quality made her an important part of the creative process, even though she wasn't publicly recognized for it.

Her home became a sanctuary for creativity. Many artists, producers, and musicians found themselves at Kim's home, whether to relax or work on projects in a calm environment. It was a space where creativity could flow freely, without the pressures of the outside world. The energy in her home was a reflection of her personality—peaceful, warm, and inspiring. Many artists who spent time there spoke about how the environment Kim created helped them focus and produce some of their best work. She understood that creativity needed the right space to grow, and she fostered that for the people in her life.

Kim also had a nurturing spirit, which naturally made her a mentor to many young artists who were just starting out in the industry. Though she wasn't a formal mentor, she offered guidance and advice to those who sought her out. Young women, in particular, looked up to her for advice on navigating the complexities of both the entertainment world and personal life. Kim never hesitated to share her experiences, both the good and the challenging, to help others learn and grow. Her influence as a mentor came from her ability to relate to people on a human level, understanding their struggles and offering them genuine support.

Beyond her immediate circle, Kim also played a role in helping Diddy discover and nurture new talent. She had a natural ability to spot potential in artists, and her opinion mattered when Diddy was scouting for the next big act. Whether it was helping to evaluate demo tapes or offering thoughts on an up-and-coming artist, her feedback was invaluable. Her understanding of what made an artist truly connect with audiences allowed her to offer unique perspectives. Diddy often acknowledged that Kim's influence helped him shape some of his biggest projects, making her an essential part of his creative process.

Kim's involvement in the creative process also extended to visuals. She had a keen eye for aesthetics, and her background in modelling gave her a unique understanding of how music videos, album covers, and promotional materials should look. Her input was often sought when it came to designing the visual components of an artist's work. She helped ensure that the image and style matched the music, creating a cohesive and powerful presentation. This was another example of how her influence reached beyond her personal relationships, impacting the industry at large.

Kim Porter was the unsung hero behind some of the biggest moments in music during her time. She didn't seek out recognition for her contributions, but those who knew her understood the depth of her influence. Whether it was through providing feedback, offering emotional support, or creating a space where creativity could thrive, Kim's role in the industry was vital. Her ability to quietly influence the creative process and support artists, without seeking the spotlight, is a testament to her strength and generosity.

# CHAPTER 6

# Fashion, Beauty, and Business

K im Porter's entrepreneurial spirit came to life when she launched her unisex hair care brand, **Three Brown Girls**. This brand was a reflection of her passion for beauty and her desire to empower others through self-expression. It was also a personal endeavor that stemmed from her own experiences and struggles with hair care, especially when it came to finding products that worked well for multicultural hair textures. The creation of Three Brown Girls was more than a business move; it was a way for Kim to help others feel confident and beautiful, just as she had always aspired to do through her work in the fashion and entertainment industries.

## The Inspiration Behind the Brand

The idea for Three Brown Girls was born out of Kim's deep understanding of the unique challenges faced by people with diverse hair types, especially women of color. Throughout her modelling career, Kim had experienced firsthand how the beauty industry often lacked products designed specifically for multicultural hair. She knew that many women struggled to find products that not only enhanced the health of their hair but also embraced its natural beauty. This realization fueled her drive to create a line that would address these needs in a meaningful and inclusive way.

Kim saw an opportunity to fill a gap in the market. Her own journey with hair care, combined with the stories she heard from friends and fellow models, pushed her to create products that catered to a wide range of hair textures. She was committed to offering something that would allow people to embrace their natural hair, without feeling the pressure to conform to mainstream beauty standards.

## Building the Brand

Creating Three Brown Girls was not an overnight process. Kim approached the project with the same dedication and work ethic she brought to her modelling and acting careers. She knew that to create a successful brand, she needed more than just a great idea—she needed the right team, the right formulas, and a clear vision for what her brand would represent. This was not just a business venture for her; it was a personal mission to empower individuals, particularly women of color, by providing them with high-quality, effective hair care products.

Kim partnered with experts in the beauty and hair care industries to develop formulas that would work for a variety of hair types. She was deeply involved in the development process, ensuring that each product met her high standards. Her hands-on approach allowed her to create a brand that was not only effective but also authentic. Kim wanted every customer to feel confident that they were using products that were created with care, knowledge, and love.

Three Brown Girls was designed to be a brand that celebrated diversity and self-expression. Kim wanted her customers to feel proud of their hair, regardless of its texture or type. This message of empowerment and self-love was at the core of her brand, and it resonated with many people who had long felt overlooked by the beauty industry.

## The Product Line

The product line for Three Brown Girls was carefully curated to address the specific needs of multicultural hair. Kim wanted to ensure that her products were not only versatile but also nourishing. She understood that maintaining healthy hair often required a delicate balance of moisture, strength, and protection, especially for textured hair, which can be more prone to dryness and breakage.

One of the standout products in the line was a deep-conditioning treatment that was formulated to hydrate and repair damaged hair. This product became a favorite among customers because it was effective for various hair types, from curly to coily to wavy. The formula was designed to penetrate the hair shaft, providing moisture and nutrients to restore the hair's natural strength and shine.

Kim also focused on creating a styling cream that allowed for versatility. Whether customers wanted to wear their hair in natural curls, twist-outs, or sleek styles, the styling cream offered flexibility without compromising hair health. This product became a staple for many women who wanted to style their hair while maintaining its natural integrity.

In addition to these products, Kim was passionate about developing a scalp treatment that would promote healthy hair growth. She understood that healthy hair starts with a healthy scalp, and this product addressed common issues like dryness, itchiness, and irritation. The scalp treatment became a must-have for many customers who were looking to improve their hair from the roots.

## A Personal Mission

For Kim Porter, Three Brown Girls was not just about selling hair care products—it was about building a community. She wanted her brand to be a space where people could come together to celebrate their natural beauty and support one another. Through her brand, she aimed to challenge traditional beauty standards and encourage people to embrace what made them unique.

This personal mission was deeply connected to Kim's own journey. Throughout her life, she had learned the importance of self-love and self-acceptance, and she wanted to share that message with others. She knew that beauty was more than skin deep, and she believed that when people felt good about themselves, they were able to thrive in all areas of their lives.

Kim often shared her personal hair care tips and routines with her customers, offering them guidance on how to take care of their hair and feel their best. She wanted her brand to be a source of empowerment, and she was always willing to engage with her customers and provide them with the support they needed.

## The Impact of Three Brown Girls

Three Brown Girls quickly gained a loyal following, particularly among women of colour who had long been searching for products that catered to their specific needs. Kim's dedication to quality and authenticity resonated with her customers, and her brand became a trusted name in the beauty industry. The brand's emphasis on inclusivity and self-expression also attracted a diverse range of customers, many of whom felt seen and valued by the brand's message.

Kim's influence extended beyond the products themselves. Through Three Brown Girls, she became a role model for aspiring entrepreneurs and women who wanted to take control of their own beauty narratives. Her success showed others that it was possible to build a business that was not only profitable but also meaningful.

The impact of Three Brown Girls went beyond the shelves of beauty stores. It was part of a larger movement in the beauty industry that celebrated diversity and challenged outdated beauty standards. Kim Porter played a significant role in this movement, using her platform to uplift others and create products that made people feel proud of who they were.

### A Legacy

Although Kim Porter is no longer with us, her legacy lives on through Three Brown Girls and the countless people she inspired. Her brand continues to be a symbol of empowerment and self-love, reminding people to embrace their natural beauty and take pride in their individuality. Kim's entrepreneurial spirit, combined with her passion for helping others, has left a lasting impact on the beauty industry and on the lives of her customers.

Three Brown Girls is more than just a hair care brand—it is a testament to Kim Porter's vision, determination, and love for her community. Through her brand, she has created a space where people can celebrate who they are and feel confident in their own skin.

# Her Love for Fashion and Beauty

Kim Porter's love for fashion and beauty was a defining aspect of her life. Even from a young age, she had a natural eye for style, combining elegance with a personal touch that made her stand out. Growing up in Columbus, Georgia, fashion was an expression of her personality, and she often used her creativity to put together outfits that reflected her inner confidence. This love for fashion only grew stronger as she pursued a career in modelling and gained exposure to the industry's top designers and trends.

When she moved to New York to break into modelling, Kim found herself immersed in a world where fashion was not just a passion but a way of life. New York City, with its fast-paced, ever-changing fashion scene, became the backdrop for Kim's growth as a model and a style icon. She graced the covers of magazines and worked with top brands, but more than just following trends, Kim developed her own distinct sense of style. Her looks were always polished, sophisticated, and effortlessly chic.

One of Kim's strengths was her ability to blend high fashion with everyday wear, making her style accessible and relatable. Whether she was attending glamorous events with Sean "Diddy" Combs or spending time with her children, she had a unique way of bringing beauty into her daily life. Her wardrobe was a reflection of her diverse tastes, featuring everything from couture gowns to casual yet stylish streetwear. Kim knew how to balance bold, fashion-forward pieces with timeless classics, a skill that many admired.

Her beauty routine was equally important to her as her fashion sense. Kim took great care in her appearance, ensuring that her skin, hair, and makeup always looked flawless. She embraced natural beauty and often emphasized simplicity in her look. While she was known to experiment with different hairstyles and makeup trends, Kim always made sure that her appearance remained authentic and true to who she was.

Kim's love for beauty extended to her entrepreneurial ventures, where she turned her passion into a platform for helping others. She was committed to creating beauty products that catered to women of color, who often struggled to find products suited to their unique needs. This passion led to her launching her hair care line, **Three Brown Girls**, which became an important part of her legacy in the beauty industry.

Kim understood that beauty was not just about physical appearance but also about self-expression and confidence. She believed that feeling good on the outside could positively influence how a person feels on the inside. Through her fashion choices and beauty rituals, she embodied this belief, inspiring others to embrace their own sense of style and beauty.

# Empowering Other Women Through Her Business Ventures

Kim Porter's entrepreneurial spirit was rooted in her desire to empower other women, particularly women of color. After years of working in the entertainment and fashion industries, she realized that there was a gap in the market for beauty products designed specifically for multicultural hair textures. Kim knew firsthand the challenges women of color faced when trying to find products that catered to their needs, and she wanted to make a difference.

The creation of **Three Brown Girls**, her hair care line, was a direct response to these challenges. Kim didn't just want to create a brand; she wanted to build a movement. Her goal was to empower women to feel confident in their natural beauty, no matter their hair type or texture. By providing products that addressed the specific needs of multicultural women, Kim helped her customers embrace their natural beauty with pride. The hair care line offered a range of products designed to nourish and enhance natural hair, from shampoos and conditioners to styling creams and treatments.

Through her business ventures, Kim aimed to encourage women to take control of their beauty routines in a way that celebrated their uniqueness. She understood the importance of representation in the beauty industry and wanted to create products that reflected the diversity of her customer base. **Three Brown Girls** was not just about selling products; it was about creating a sense of community and support for women who often felt overlooked by mainstream beauty brands.

Kim believed that by providing high-quality beauty products tailored to women of color, she could help boost their confidence. She was passionate about encouraging women to embrace their natural hair and not feel pressured to conform to traditional beauty standards that didn't reflect their cultural heritage. This empowerment was at the heart of her brand's mission, and it resonated deeply with her customers.

Beyond her products, Kim was known for offering advice and support to other women looking to break into the beauty or fashion industries. She used her platform to mentor young women, sharing her experiences and helping them navigate the challenges of entrepreneurship. Kim was a strong advocate for women supporting women, and she often emphasized the importance of collaboration over competition. She believed that when women uplift one another, they can achieve great things together.

Her influence went beyond her own brand. Kim was often seen as a role model for other women of color who aspired to launch their own businesses. She demonstrated that success was possible with hard work, vision, and a commitment to empowering others. Her entrepreneurial journey inspired many women to take their own steps toward achieving financial independence and personal fulfillment.

Kim's business ventures were also deeply personal. As a mother, she wanted to create a legacy that her children could be proud of, and her work with **Three Brown Girls** was a reflection of that. She hoped to teach her children, particularly her daughters, the importance of self-confidence, self-care, and entrepreneurship. By involving them in her business and showing them the value of hard work, Kim passed down valuable lessons that would shape their future.

Her work in the beauty industry highlighted her belief that beauty goes beyond surface-level appearances. She saw it as a tool for empowerment, helping women feel strong, capable, and confident in their own skin. Through her products and her influence, Kim was able to make a lasting impact on the lives of countless women.

# CHAPTER 7

# Friendships and Giving Back

Kim Porter was well-known for her warmth and ability to form deep, genuine friendships, particularly with people in the entertainment industry. Despite the demands of her career and her relationships, Kim always made time for the people she cared about. Many of her closest friends were high-profile figures, yet the bond they shared with her transcended the typical superficial friendships often seen in celebrity circles. Those who knew her best spoke of her loyalty, kindness, and how she nurtured long-lasting connections.

One of Kim's most enduring friendships was with **Mary J. Blige**, the iconic singer known as the "Queen of Hip-Hop Soul." The two women met early in their careers and quickly became inseparable. Their friendship wasn't just based on shared industry experiences; they supported each other through personal ups and downs, including heartbreaks, career challenges, and family issues. Mary often credited Kim with helping her navigate difficult times, describing her as more than just a friend but as a sister. Kim's advice, emotional support, and ability to listen without judgment made her an invaluable part of Mary's life.

Another important friendship in Kim's life was with **Beyoncé**. While Beyoncé is known for keeping her circle tight, Kim was someone she considered a close and trusted friend. They met through mutual friends in the music industry, and their connection grew over the years. What stood out to many about their friendship was how grounded it remained despite their fame. They often spent time together privately, sharing personal milestones, celebrating successes, and supporting each other's ventures. Beyoncé has spoken in interviews about how Kim's presence in her life brought a sense of peace and understanding that was rare in the fast-paced world of entertainment.

Kim also had a close bond with **Tracey Edmonds**, a producer and businesswoman. Both women were involved in various aspects of entertainment, but their connection was rooted in their shared experiences as mothers and entrepreneurs. They frequently exchanged advice on balancing career ambitions with the responsibilities of motherhood. Kim's nurturing nature was often evident in these relationships, and her friends appreciated her willingness to help without expecting anything in return. Tracey once mentioned that Kim had a unique way of making everyone feel seen and valued, whether they were struggling or celebrating success.

Throughout her life, Kim was also known for her friendship with **Naomi Campbell**, the legendary supermodel. Both women shared the experience of working in the fashion industry, and their connection grew through shared experiences in modelling. Naomi often turned to Kim for advice and support, as both navigated their careers and personal lives in the public eye. Kim's ability to empathize with others, combined with her own experience in the fashion world, made her a valuable confidante to Naomi. Their friendship was marked by mutual respect and admiration for each other's strengths, both professionally and personally.

One of the most significant aspects of Kim's friendships was her **emotional intelligence**. She had an innate ability to connect with people on a deeper level, understanding their struggles and offering support in meaningful ways. This emotional intelligence made her the kind of friend that others turned to in times of need. Whether it was offering advice, lending an ear, or simply being a calming presence, Kim was the type of friend who made those around her feel better about themselves and their situations. Her friends often remarked on how grounded she remained, even while surrounded by the chaos and pressures of celebrity life.

Beyond her relationships with celebrities, Kim cultivated strong friendships with people behind the scenes in the entertainment industry. **Producers, managers, and stylists** all spoke about how much they valued Kim's kindness and generosity. She never looked at people for their status or what they could offer her, but rather connected with them on a personal level. Many of these friendships were formed during her early days in New York, when she was just starting out in the fashion industry. Even as her fame grew, Kim remained loyal to these early friends, often crediting them with helping her stay grounded.

One thing that stood out about Kim's friendships was her **ability to maintain genuine connections**, even as her own life became more complex. While fame often changes people's relationships, Kim worked hard to keep her friendships strong. She was known for throwing intimate gatherings and dinners, where she would bring together close friends to share in special moments. These gatherings were less about flashy events and more about spending quality time with the people she cared about. Her friends appreciated how, even amidst her busy life, Kim made time to nurture her relationships.

**Diddy**, her long-term partner and the father of three of her children, often spoke about how much he admired Kim's friendships. He described how her friends would frequently turn to her for advice and support because she had a way of making people feel safe and understood. Her ability to foster lasting connections wasn't just limited to her immediate circle but extended to many people in the industry who looked up to her. Diddy often remarked that Kim was the glue that held many friendships together, always making sure people felt loved and cared for.

Another important element of Kim's friendships was her **commitment to uplifting other women**. She was known for supporting her female friends, both personally and professionally. Whether it was cheering on their latest achievements or helping them through difficult times, Kim was always there to lift others up. She understood the pressures that women in the entertainment industry faced and worked hard to create a supportive network where her friends could thrive. This commitment to supporting other women made her an inspiration to many and cemented her legacy as someone who valued friendship and loyalty above all else.

Her passing in 2018 left a deep void in the lives of those who were close to her. Many of her friends, including Mary J. Blige, Beyoncé, and Naomi Campbell, shared emotional tributes, speaking about how much Kim meant to them. They remembered her as someone who was always there, offering love, support, and wisdom when they needed it most. While her life was cut short, her influence on her friends continues to be felt, and the memories they shared with her remain a lasting testament to the depth of their friendships.

# Her Generosity and Quiet Acts of Kindness

Kim Porter was known for her humble spirit, often offering her time, resources, and love without seeking the spotlight. Her generosity wasn't about grand gestures but about the small, meaningful ways she connected with people around her. Those closest to her often spoke of her ability to make people feel seen and cared for. Whether she was helping a close friend through a difficult time or supporting someone quietly behind the scenes, Kim made it clear that giving back was deeply embedded in her character.

One of the most remarkable things about Kim's kindness was how she approached it without any expectation of recognition. In the entertainment industry, where people often strive to stay in the limelight, she took a different path. Kim's generosity often took place away from cameras, and those who benefited from her kindness frequently spoke about how she never publicized her efforts. She wasn't driven by the need for validation; instead, she found joy in simply helping others. Her ability to give with no strings attached became a defining part of her legacy.

There were countless stories shared by those in her inner circle after her passing. Close friends like Mary J. Blige, Beyoncé, and Diddy often mentioned how Kim would be the first to offer support whenever someone was going through a tough time. Whether it was sending a thoughtful message, helping organize events, or simply being there to listen, Kim made sure that people knew they could count on her. Her kindness wasn't reserved for just her celebrity friends—Kim treated everyone in her life with the same level of care and thoughtfulness.

Family members recall how she consistently gave back to her hometown in Columbus, Georgia. Although she had moved on to bigger cities and had a thriving career, she never forgot her roots. Many people from her hometown remember Kim as someone who would return and quietly donate to local causes. She didn't make a big deal out of it or expect a public thank you. This dedication to helping her community, even from afar, is one of the many ways she left a lasting impact.

Kim's generosity extended beyond financial support. She was someone who offered emotional care to those around her, especially to women and young girls who looked up to her. Despite her success in modelling and entertainment, Kim was approachable and down-to-earth. She was often described as a big sister to many young women, providing advice on navigating the entertainment world, relationships, and motherhood. These moments of mentorship were invaluable to those who had the privilege of learning from her. Kim believed in lifting others up and was committed to helping people, especially women of color, find their way in industries where they were often overlooked.

## Influence on Her Children

Kim's children often spoke of how she led by example, teaching them to be kind and considerate through her actions rather than words. For Kim, kindness wasn't just about donating money or giving material gifts—it was about truly caring for people. She taught her children to treat others with respect, regardless of their background or status.

Her eldest son, Quincy Brown, once shared how his mother's spirit of generosity was something that shaped him as a person. Despite growing up in a world filled with fame and privilege, Quincy was raised with a strong sense of humility. Kim ensured that her children understood the value of hard work and the importance of staying grounded. She regularly reminded them that fame should never get in the way of helping others. Quincy has followed in his mother's footsteps by giving back to his community, often participating in charity events and advocating for mental health awareness.

Christian Combs, her son with Sean "Diddy" Combs, also spoke of how Kim's quiet acts of kindness inspired him. Christian shared that his mother always made time for others, no matter how busy she was. Whether it was helping a neighbor or supporting someone going through a tough time, Kim made sure her children witnessed these moments. Christian often reflected on how his mother taught him the importance of loyalty and being there for family and friends. He now carries this lesson with him in both his personal and professional life.

Her twin daughters, D'Lila Star and Jessie James were young when Kim passed, but her influence on them continues to grow as they mature. Diddy, their father, often shared how Kim's spirit lives on in their daughters, especially in how they care for others and treat people around them. The twins are already following in their mother's footsteps, showing a natural inclination toward kindness and empathy.

**Specific Acts of Kindness**

One memorable act of kindness that many close friends shared after Kim's passing was her support during difficult times. Kim had a reputation for being the person people turned to in moments of need. She didn't wait for public moments to show her support—she reached out privately, offering comfort in whatever way she could. Many of her celebrity friends have spoken about how she helped them through personal challenges without seeking any recognition for her efforts.

For example, Mary J. Blige, one of Kim's close friends, shared a touching story about how Kim supported her during a particularly tough period in her life. Mary was going through personal struggles and was hesitant to reach out to anyone. Kim, sensing that her friend needed someone, showed up unannounced, offering her presence and a shoulder to lean on. This small but significant gesture was a hallmark of Kim's kindness—she didn't ask if help was needed, she simply gave it, knowing that her friend would benefit from it.

Kim was also known for her charitable contributions, often supporting causes related to women and children. She regularly donated to shelters for women escaping domestic violence and supported programs that helped young girls gain access to education. These contributions weren't something she advertised or even talked about frequently. Many of her donations were made anonymously, as she preferred to help without drawing attention to herself. Kim believed in the power of quiet generosity, where the act of giving was more important than being recognized for it.

In addition to her financial donations, Kim also dedicated time to mentoring young women, especially those trying to break into the modelling and entertainment industries. She understood the challenges that came with being a woman of color in these spaces and wanted to use her experience to uplift others. Kim often invited aspiring models to her home, offering advice and guidance on how to navigate the industry with confidence and integrity. She wasn't just offering career tips—she was helping these young women build self-esteem and resilience, traits that would serve them in every aspect of their lives.

Another significant aspect of Kim's kindness was her approach to parenting, not just with her own children but with others as well. Friends of the family often shared how Kim opened her home to their children, treating them like her own. She believed that every child deserved love and attention, and she often went out of her way to create a safe, nurturing environment for the young people in her life. Whether it was hosting playdates, organizing family events, or simply making sure everyone felt included, Kim's home was known as a place of warmth and care.

Her kindness extended beyond her circle of friends and family. There are numerous stories of Kim helping people she didn't know personally. For instance, she was known to support struggling single mothers by quietly paying for their groceries or helping cover school fees for their children. These acts of kindness were never publicized or shared widely, but they had a profound impact on those who received her help. She made a difference in people's lives without expecting anything in return.

Kim Porter's generosity and acts of kindness have left a legacy, especially in the hearts of those she loved and helped. She didn't just give in material ways—she gave her time, her energy, and her love to those who needed it most. Whether it was supporting her children, lifting young women, or helping friends through difficult times, Kim's life was a testament to the power of quiet kindness. Her legacy continues to inspire her children, friends, and the countless others whose lives she touched with her generosity.

Her children now carry her values forward, living with the same sense of empathy and care that Kim demonstrated throughout her life. The ripple effect of her kindness is still felt, and her influence remains strong in the lives of those who knew her.

# How She Supported Her Community and Loved Ones

Kim Porter's commitment to her community and loved ones was rooted in her upbringing. Growing up in Columbus, Georgia, Kim was raised with a strong sense of family and loyalty. These values stayed with her throughout her life, and she consistently demonstrated her dedication to her loved ones and those who needed her support. One of the most important ways Kim supported her family was through her unwavering presence. No matter how busy her career became, she made it a priority to be present for her children, friends, and family.

Her family, especially her children, always came first. Kim was a devoted mother to Quincy, Christian, D'Lila Star, and Jessie James. She wasn't just a mother in title, but in action. Kim was known for being actively involved in her children's lives, from attending school events to helping them navigate their paths in the entertainment industry. She made sure they felt supported and grounded, despite the fame and public attention they experienced. Her ability to balance her career with her role as a mother was a testament to her deep love and commitment to her family.

Kim's relationship with her longtime partner, Sean "Diddy" Combs, further illustrated her dedication to her loved ones. Though their romantic relationship went through ups and downs, Kim remained a strong support system for Diddy, even after they separated. The two co-parented their children with mutual respect and care, and Kim often stepped in to ensure their children always had stability, despite their complex family dynamics. Her commitment to Diddy's well-being, and to maintaining a healthy environment for their children, was widely recognized and respected.

Beyond her immediate family, Kim's community extended to her friends and even to those in need whom she didn't know personally. She was known for reaching out to friends in difficult times, offering whatever support she could—whether emotional or material. Her friends often shared stories about how Kim made time to be there for them, even when her schedule was packed. She had a remarkable ability to listen and empathize, making her a confidante to many people in her circle.

Another key aspect of how Kim supported her community was through her philanthropic efforts. Though she wasn't the type to boast about her charitable contributions, Kim quietly supported several causes, especially those benefiting women and children. She believed in giving back, and many of her friends and family remember how she would donate to causes that aligned with her values. Her impact wasn't always loud, but it was deeply felt by those who benefited from her generosity.

Kim's acts of kindness weren't limited to financial contributions. She often used her platform to advocate for change in the fashion and entertainment industries, particularly in pushing for more diversity. She supported young Black women who were entering the modelling and acting world, often mentoring them and giving them advice on how to navigate the challenges they might face. Kim believed in creating opportunities for others and was always willing to share her knowledge and experiences to help others succeed.

Kim Porter exemplified what it meant to support her community and loved ones. Whether through acts of kindness, emotional support, or simply being present, she left an indelible mark on the people around her. Her quiet generosity and strong sense of loyalty continue to be remembered and celebrated by those who knew her. Even after her passing, the ripple effect of her kindness lives on, carried forward by her children, friends, and the countless lives she touched.

# CHAPTER 8

# Saying Goodbye

Kim Porter's passing on November 15, 2018, marked an unforgettable day in the lives of her family, friends, and many admirers around the world. She was only 47 years old, and her death left an enormous emotional impact on those closest to her. That day started like any other, but soon, the news of her sudden passing spread, sending shockwaves through the entertainment industry and beyond.

On that fateful day, Kim Porter was found unresponsive in her Los Angeles home. Initial reports suggested that she had been suffering from flu-like symptoms for several weeks. Those who knew her had no idea that something so serious was about to happen. The official cause of death was later revealed to be lobar pneumonia, a severe lung infection. While the medical facts offered some answers, they did little to soften the grief felt by her family and friends.

The news of Kim's passing broke publicly shortly after her death, with sources close to the family confirming it to the media. For many, the idea of someone so full of life being gone was hard to grasp. She was not only a model and actress but, more importantly, a mother, friend, and deeply beloved figure in the entertainment industry. Her sudden departure left many speechless.

For Sean "Diddy" Combs, Kim's former partner and father to three of her children, the loss was overwhelming. Though the two were no longer romantically involved, they had shared more than a decade together and remained close friends. Their relationship had evolved into a deep and supportive bond, especially when it came to co-parenting their children. Diddy was reportedly devastated by the news. In the days following her passing, he described Kim as his soulmate and the person who had been there for him during some of the most challenging moments of his life. Their relationship was one built on respect and care, even after their romantic ties had ended. His grief was evident, and his tribute to Kim became one of the most heartfelt moments following her death.

Kim's children, Quincy, Christian, D'Lila, and Jessie, faced an immeasurable loss. The heartache of losing a mother at such a young age is something no one can fully prepare for. Quincy, her oldest son from her relationship with Al B. Sure! shared an emotional tribute on social media, expressing his deep love for his mother and the pain of her passing. Christian, who was incredibly close to Kim, also took to social media to honor her, remembering her as not only a mother but also as his best friend. The twins, D'Lila and Jessie, were just 12 years old when their mother passed, and they too paid tribute to her in the weeks following her death, with the help of their father and older siblings. The outpouring of love from her children was a clear reflection of how much Kim meant to them.

In the days that followed, countless tributes poured in from friends, family, and celebrities. Kim Porter was not just admired for her beauty and career, but for her kindness, warmth, and spirit. Friends described her as someone who made everyone around her feel loved and valued. She had an infectious smile and a gentle presence that made people feel at ease. Mary J. Blige, Beyoncé, and many other close friends shared touching memories of Kim, focusing on her compassion and the positive energy she brought into every room she entered.

One of the most striking aspects of the grief that followed Kim's death was the way her passing brought people together. Her memorial service, held in her hometown of Columbus, Georgia, was a beautiful celebration of her life. Hundreds of people gathered to honor her, including many high-profile figures in the entertainment world. The service was not just a moment to mourn her loss but also a chance to celebrate her life, the joy she brought to others, and the love she gave to her children and friends. Diddy gave a heartfelt eulogy, speaking through his tears about the profound influence Kim had on his life and the lives of their children. He shared memories of their time together, emphasizing how much she had taught him about love, family, and friendship.

In the months following her death, Diddy continued to honor Kim's legacy. He made sure that their children were surrounded by love and support during such a difficult time. On social media, he often shared pictures and memories of Kim, ensuring that her presence was still felt, even in her absence. Diddy's deep grief was evident, but so was his resolve to carry on Kim's legacy, particularly for their children.

The grief extended far beyond her immediate family. The entertainment industry felt her loss. Kim was a quiet force behind many successful people, offering them advice, support, and love. Her ability to lift others up, even when she wasn't in the spotlight, was something that many admired. People often spoke about how she was the type of person who made others feel important, whether they were celebrities or someone working behind the scenes.

As time passed, the deep sorrow surrounding her death has slowly turned into a celebration of her life. Her family continues to keep her memory alive. On special occasions, such as her birthday or the anniversary of her passing, her children and Diddy share personal tributes, showing that Kim's presence is still felt every day. For them, her legacy is not just in her career or public persona but in the love and values she instilled in them.

Kim Porter's death was a tragedy, but her life remains an inspiration to many. The grief that followed her passing is a testament to how much she was loved and how deeply she impacted the lives of those around her. While she is no longer physically present, her spirit lives on through her children, her friends, and the countless people she touched during her life.

# Tributes from Family, Friends, and Celebrities

When Kim Porter passed away in November 2018, it left a deep void in the lives of those who loved and admired her. Her death, sudden and unexpected, was met with an outpouring of grief from family members, close friends, and celebrities. The tributes that poured in after her passing reflected the immense love and respect people had for her, not just as a public figure but as a deeply compassionate and generous individual.

Sean "Diddy" Combs, who shared three children with Kim and remained close to her even after their romantic relationship ended, was perhaps the most affected by her passing. In his public tributes, Diddy spoke about Kim as more than just a former partner or co-parent. She was his best friend, his confidante, and someone who had been by his side for much of his life. Diddy shared several emotional posts on social media, calling Kim "more than a soulmate" and remembering her as the person who completed him. In the days following her death, he posted heartfelt messages, including videos of family moments, revealing the depth of his grief and the void her loss had left in his life.

Diddy also organized an elaborate and moving celebration of Kim's life, gathering their children, friends, and other loved ones for a memorial service. He ensured that Kim's memory was honored in the grandest way, showing how much she meant to him and the family they shared. The memorial service was filled with emotional speeches, music, and reflections from those who knew her best, a testament to how cherished she was.

Her children, Quincy Brown, Christian Combs, and twin daughters, D'Lila Star and Jessie James, were devastated by the loss of their mother. Quincy, her eldest son, who Kim had from a previous relationship with singer Al B. Sure!, paid tribute by reflecting on the unconditional love she had given him throughout his life. He shared stories of how she supported him in every decision he made and how she was the glue that held their family together. Christian, Kim and Diddy's son, also posted messages celebrating his mother's life, describing her as his rock and his biggest supporter. The twins, though younger, were equally affected by the loss, and their father and older siblings rallied around them to provide comfort and love.

Beyond her immediate family, Kim's passing was felt deeply by her close circle of friends. She had cultivated lasting friendships in the entertainment industry, with people like Mary J. Blige, Beyoncé, and Naomi Campbell. Mary J. Blige, who had been one of Kim's closest friends for decades, shared an emotional tribute. She described Kim as someone who had always been there for her through thick and thin, whether in moments of joy or hardship. Blige noted Kim's kind, giving nature, saying that she had the ability to uplift and support everyone around her.

Beyoncé, who had also known Kim for many years, posted a touching tribute on her website. Alongside a beautiful photograph of Kim, Beyoncé wrote a simple yet powerful message: "Heaven couldn't wait for you." It was clear from these tributes that Kim's friendships were deep and meaningful, characterized by mutual respect and love.

Naomi Campbell also honored Kim's memory, describing her as "an earth angel." In a heartfelt post,

Naomi spoke of their close friendship and the incredible light that Kim brought to everyone's life. Campbell mentioned that Kim was one of the most selfless people she had ever known, always putting others before herself, and noted how much she would be missed by her friends and loved ones.

Kim's generosity and warmth extended far beyond her famous friends. She was beloved by many in the industry for her down-to-earth personality and her willingness to lend a helping hand. Countless others who had worked with Kim over the years—from models and stylists to photographers and producers—shared their own memories of her, all echoing the same sentiment: Kim was a rare soul who touched the hearts of everyone she met. Many mentioned her infectious smile and the way she made people feel special, whether in a professional or personal setting.

The entertainment industry was also deeply impacted by her passing. Celebrities who had interacted with Kim through the years—such as Rihanna, 50 Cent, and Missy Elliott—shared their grief on social media. Rihanna wrote a tribute highlighting Kim's role as an inspiration, not just for her beauty and grace but for her strength and devotion as a mother. She noted how much she admired Kim's ability to balance her family life with the pressures of being in the public eye.

For Diddy, Kim's death marked a significant turning point in his life. He continued to honor her memory by regularly posting tributes on social media, celebrating her on important dates such as her birthday and Mother's Day. In one particularly moving post, he shared that losing Kim made him realize the importance of love and family, urging others to appreciate their loved ones while they still have the chance.

The impact of Kim's passing on her loved ones was profound. She had been the center of her family, the person who brought everyone together, and her absence left a void that could never be filled. For her children, especially, losing their mother was an experience they would carry for the rest of their lives. In the months following her death, Diddy often spoke about how he was trying to stay strong for their kids and how the family was adjusting to life without Kim. He took on the role of both mother and father, ensuring that their children continued to feel the love and support that Kim had always provided.

In a world where people are often judged by their public image, Kim Porter was remembered for something far more valuable—her heart. Her passing reminded everyone of the importance of kindness, love, and the connections we share with those around us. She left behind a legacy of love, not only in the lives of her children and family but also in the hearts of the many people she touched during her time on earth. Her spirit lives on through the countless tributes, memories, and stories shared by those who were fortunate enough to know her.

# The Impact of Kim Porter's Death on Her Loved Ones

When Kim Porter passed away on November 15, 2018, it sent shockwaves through the lives of those who knew and loved her. For many, Kim was not just a public figure, but a mother, a best friend, and a guiding force in their lives. Her sudden passing due to complications from pneumonia left a deep and profound impact on her family, friends, and the entertainment world. The grief was overwhelming, but her legacy of love and strength continues to shape the lives of those closest to her.

For her children, Kim was the pillar of their lives. Quincy Brown, Christian Combs, and twin daughters D'Lila Star and Jessie James all looked to their mother as their source of stability and unconditional love. The loss of a mother at any age is deeply painful, but for Kim's children, it was especially hard. They had always been close, and she was known to be very hands-on in their lives. Whether it was through cooking meals, being present for important milestones, or guiding them through personal challenges, Kim was the glue that held the family together.

After her passing, her children shared touching tributes to her. Quincy, her eldest son, often reflected on how much his mother shaped his character. In interviews and public statements, he expressed his deep admiration for her wisdom and grace. He credited Kim for teaching him to be strong yet kind and to always hold onto the values of family. For Quincy, the loss of his mother was not just the loss of a parent but the loss of someone who was his rock. He has frequently spoken about how her influence continues to guide him as he navigates his own career in the entertainment industry.

Christian Combs, Kim's son with Sean "Diddy" Combs, was similarly impacted. Growing up, Christian was always close to his mother, and she was instrumental in shaping his path in music and fashion. After her passing, Christian often turned to social media to share his grief and his love for her. He frequently posted memories and pictures of their time together, sharing with the world just how much his mother meant to him. For Christian, Kim wasn't just a parent—she was his biggest supporter, always pushing him to pursue his dreams. The grief he felt after her passing was evident, but like Quincy, he has often spoken about how her memory continues to inspire him every day.

The youngest in the family, twin daughters D'Lila Star and Jessie James, were only 12 years old when their mother passed. Being at such a tender age, the impact of her death was especially hard for them. Kim had always been an incredibly devoted mother, especially to her girls. She made sure they felt loved and nurtured, despite her busy life. After her passing, it became clear just how much Kim had been involved in every aspect of their lives. Diddy, their father, stepped in to take on the dual role of both parents, but he often shared how irreplaceable Kim was in their lives. The twins continue to honor their mother through their own journeys, and her presence is still felt through the love and guidance she gave them.

For Sean "Diddy" Combs, the loss of Kim Porter was especially profound. Despite their romantic relationship ending years before her death, the two remained incredibly close friends and co-parents. Diddy often referred to Kim as his soulmate and his best friend, and after her passing, he publicly spoke about the immense grief he felt. He shared that Kim was his confidante, someone he could always rely on, and a key figure in his life. After her death, Diddy took to social media and interviews to express how much Kim meant to him, stating that losing her was the most painful experience he had ever endured. He described her as the love of his life, and even though they were no longer together, their bond remained as strong as ever.

Diddy's response to Kim's death was filled with heartfelt tributes. He organized a memorial service that brought together family and friends to celebrate Kim's life. It was clear from his actions and words that Kim's passing had left a deep void in his life. He often spoke about how he was committed to being the best father he could be to their children, stepping into a role that Kim had previously led with grace. For Diddy, the challenge was not just dealing with his own grief but helping his children navigate the immense loss they were feeling.

Kim's passing also had a significant impact on her close circle of friends. Known for her kindness and generosity, Kim had built strong relationships with many in the entertainment industry, including celebrities like Mary J. Blige, Beyoncé, and Naomi Campbell. These friendships were not just superficial connections, but deep bonds built over years of trust and shared experiences. After her passing, many of Kim's friends shared their grief publicly, offering heartfelt tributes that spoke to her impact as a friend and confidante.

Mary J. Blige was one of Kim's closest friends. After her passing, Mary shared that Kim had been like a sister to her, someone who was always there with words of encouragement and love. She recalled how Kim's spirit was one of strength and positivity, and how she was always lifting others up, even in her own times of difficulty. Beyoncé also paid tribute to Kim, posting a beautiful picture of her to honor her life. The outpouring of love from her friends showed just how deeply Kim was loved and respected in her personal and professional circles.

Kim's death also had an impact on the wider entertainment industry. As a model, actress, and entrepreneur, she had built a career that was respected by many. But more than that, it was her warmth, humility, and genuine kindness that people remembered most. The entertainment world mourned the loss of a woman who had touched so many lives, both publicly and privately. Her passing was a reminder of the fragility of life and the importance of cherishing those we love.

In the months and years following her death, Kim Porter's legacy continues to live on through her children, her friends, and those whose lives she touched. Her memory remains a powerful force in the lives of her loved ones, a constant reminder of the love and grace she embodied. Though the pain of losing her is still felt deeply, those closest to Kim find comfort in the lessons she taught them—lessons about love, family, and living life with purpose.

Kim Porter's passing left an undeniable void, but her spirit lives on through the people she loved and the lives she shaped. Her children carry forward her legacy, ensuring that her influence remains a guiding light in their journey through life.

# CHAPTER 9

# Her Legacy Lives On

Kim Porter's legacy is most evident in the lives of her four children: Quincy Brown, Christian Combs, and twin daughters D'Lila Star and Jessie James. Each of her children carries forward the values, love, and strength that she instilled in them, making sure that her memory lives on, not only through their accomplishments but through the character and grace with which they approach life. Kim was always more than just a mother—she was a guiding force for her children, and that influence is reflected in the way they navigate their personal and professional lives.

## Quincy Brown: Following in His Mother's Footsteps

Quincy Brown, Kim's firstborn, came from her relationship with singer Al B. Sure!, but he was also adopted by Sean "Diddy" Combs and raised in a blended, loving family. Quincy has made a name for himself in the entertainment industry, following in both of his parents' footsteps with a career in music, acting, and fashion. His talent and drive are a testament to the nurturing environment Kim provided. Growing up around the entertainment world, Quincy learned the importance of hard work, perseverance, and humility—values that Kim made sure to instil in all her children.

Quincy has shown an incredible ability to balance his acting and music careers, which is a reflection of the well-rounded support he received from his mother. He's known for starring in films like *Brotherly Love* and *Dope*, as well as his role in the popular TV show *Star*. His career, while impressive, is not just about the roles he plays, but how he conducts himself off-screen. Quincy often speaks about his mother's influence, noting that her love, guidance, and sense of responsibility continue to shape his approach to life and his work. Through his work in entertainment, Quincy carries forward Kim's love for creativity and her emphasis on always striving to be better, while staying grounded in family values.

Beyond his professional achievements, Quincy has maintained a deep connection to his mother's legacy by being a loving older brother and supportive figure in his family. He frequently shares photos and stories of Kim on social media, honouring her memory and keeping her spirit alive for his siblings and their extended family. Through Quincy, Kim's nurturing, loving nature remains at the heart of their family, even in her absence.


**Christian Combs: A Rising Star in Music and Fashion**

Christian Combs, the son Kim had with Diddy, has taken his own place in the spotlight, particularly in music and fashion. He has adopted the stage name King Combs and has pursued a successful career in hip-hop, following in his father's footsteps. Christian's music is a reflection of his parents' influence—his mother's grace and creativity, and his father's business acumen and legacy in the music industry. His songs often pay tribute to the 1990s hip-hop era, the golden years that Diddy helped shape, but Christian brings his own flair to the genre, making sure to honor the legacy of his family while carving out his unique identity.

Christian's rise in the fashion world is another way he carries Kim's legacy. Kim was known for her impeccable style and love for fashion, and Christian embodies that same passion. He has modelled for luxury brands like Dolce & Gabbana, and he takes pride in his personal style, much like his mother did. Kim's influence is clear in his poise, confidence, and the way he navigates both the fashion and music industries with elegance and class.

In interviews, Christian has frequently mentioned how much his mother's love and support shaped his upbringing. He has expressed that her grounding influence was crucial in helping him stay focused on his goals, despite growing up in the spotlight. Kim ensured that Christian had a strong sense of identity and purpose, and that's reflected in how he approaches his music and his public image. He also honors her legacy by being a strong and protective older brother to his twin sisters, D'Lila and Jessie.

## D'Lila Star and Jessie James: Kim's Youngest Legacy Bearers

Kim's twin daughters, D'Lila Star and Jessie James were only 12 years old when she passed away, but even at a young age, they have already shown that they carry their mother's strength and grace. The twins, who look remarkably like their mother, are often seen with their father, Sean "Diddy" Combs, attending events and growing up in the public eye. They have a quiet confidence that reflects Kim's influence, and they are frequently seen alongside their older siblings, especially Quincy and Christian, who have taken on protective roles in their lives.

Though young, D'Lila and Jessie are already following their family's path in the entertainment industry, with appearances at fashion events and the beginnings of modelling careers. Their natural beauty and elegance are a direct reflection of Kim's genes, and it's clear that they have inherited her sense of style. More importantly, the twins have been raised to understand the importance of family and values, something Kim instilled in all her children. Diddy has often spoken about how he tries to honor Kim by raising the twins in a way that keeps her memory close, ensuring that they grow up knowing how much their mother loved them.

As they grow older, D'Lila and Jessie will undoubtedly continue to represent Kim's legacy in both the fashion and entertainment industries. More than their public roles, though, the way they interact with their family and the world shows the love and lessons Kim passed down to them. They embody her kindness, strength, and sense of responsibility, ensuring that Kim's presence is still felt in the world through their actions and accomplishments.

### Honouring Kim's Memory as a Family

One of the most profound ways Kim's children continue her legacy is through the close bond they maintain as a family. Kim made it a priority to ensure her children had strong family connections, and even after her passing, that bond has remained. The children often come together on important dates—birthdays, anniversaries, and holidays—to celebrate her life. Sean "Diddy" Combs has taken it upon himself to ensure that Kim's legacy lives on through the family, often sharing personal tributes to her on social media, emphasizing the impact she had on him and their children.

The family's public tributes, while beautiful, are only a small part of how Kim's children honor her. They each carry forward the values of love, loyalty, and strength that she exemplified in her life. Kim's legacy isn't just about the careers her children pursue or the public tributes they make—it's about the way they live their lives. Whether it's Quincy's commitment to family, Christian's determination in music and fashion, or the twins' quiet strength and grace, Kim Porter's legacy lives on through her children in every step they take.

# Diddy's Ongoing Tributes and Reflections

Since Kim Porter's passing in November 2018, Sean "Diddy" Combs has continued to honor her memory in many ways. Their relationship spanned decades, filled with ups and downs, but it was rooted in love and deep friendship. Diddy has been vocal about the profound impact Kim had on his life, both as the mother of his children and as a close confidante. Even after their romantic relationship ended, Diddy often referred to Kim as his "best friend," and her passing left a significant void in his life.

## A Lasting Friendship and Co-Parenting Journey

Though their romantic relationship had its challenges, Kim and Diddy always prioritized their children and maintained a strong co-parenting partnership. Diddy has frequently mentioned how Kim was more than just a mother to their children; she was his guide, his source of strength, and his closest companion. Even after they separated as a couple, the bond between them remained unbreakable, as they co-parented Quincy, Christian, and their twin daughters, D'Lila Star and Jessie James. In his reflections, Diddy often speaks about how Kim helped him become the father he is today, pushing him to be more present and nurturing.

Her influence on their family dynamic is something Diddy regularly acknowledges. He has shared that despite his busy career, Kim always ensured the children had structure, love, and consistency at home. Diddy's tributes reflect how much he admired Kim's ability to keep their family grounded, even when life was chaotic. He often speaks about her role in keeping the family strong, noting that she was the heart and glue of their family.

## Public Tributes and Personal Reflections

In the years since Kim's death, Diddy has used social media and interviews to publicly express his love and grief. On what would have been Kim's 50th birthday in December 2020, Diddy shared a heartfelt Instagram post, writing, "HAPPY BIRTHDAY KIM!!! We love you and we miss you!!!" Accompanied by photos of their family, the post was an emotional tribute to Kim's legacy as a mother and partner. Diddy's reflections are often raw and honest, as he expresses how much he still feels her absence in his life.

Each anniversary of Kim's passing has also been marked by Diddy sharing his thoughts on social media, often accompanied by photos and videos of their life together. He speaks candidly about his grief and the lessons he continues to learn from her, even after her death. In one post, he wrote, "I've been trying to wake up out of this nightmare, but I haven't. I don't know what I'm going to do without you, baby. I miss you so much."

Diddy's reflections often touch on how Kim's death forced him to rethink his priorities. He has openly talked about how her passing made him slow down and focus more on his family. In interviews, he mentioned how Kim's love for their children has inspired him to be more involved in their lives. He often speaks about feeling her presence and being guided by her in how he raises their children. Her influence remains a guiding force in his parenting, even in her absence.

## Tributes to Kim's Motherhood

Diddy's tributes also highlight Kim's exceptional role as a mother. He often describes her as the perfect mother, someone who gave everything for her children. Her nurturing and selfless nature left a lasting impression not only on her children but also on Diddy, who frequently reflects on how much she gave of herself to their family.

In a moving tribute on Mother's Day, Diddy shared a photo of Kim and their children, writing, "This Mother's Day will be hard for me, but I'm holding on to the precious memories." He described how much their children miss her and how they keep her memory alive by talking about her every day. His posts about Kim on Mother's Day show how much he appreciated her dedication to motherhood and how she balanced that role with her own career and interests.

Diddy's reflections often emphasize that no one could replace the love and care Kim provided. Her presence in their children's lives was monumental, and Diddy continues to ensure that her influence is felt in their day-to-day experiences. He has spoken about how he and the children keep her memory alive by celebrating her life, and he ensures that the children know how proud she was of them.

## A Tribute Through Fatherhood

Since Kim's passing, Diddy has taken on a more active role in his children's lives. He has expressed how Kim's love for their kids continues to inspire him to be a better father. In interviews, Diddy has shared that losing Kim made him realize how short life can be and how important it is to be present for the people you love. He often speaks about how Kim's lessons in parenting guide him, especially when it comes to showing their children love, support, and understanding.

In the months following her death, Diddy took to social media to express how he was learning to balance his demanding career with being a full-time dad. In a candid post, he shared, "I'm just a father now. Every day, I wake up trying to figure out how to raise these girls without Kim." His reflections often convey his deep sense of responsibility, as he carries on the parenting journey they once shared.

He has also talked about the difficulties of filling the void left by Kim, especially for their daughters. Diddy frequently reflects on how much his twin girls miss their mother, and he works to ensure they always feel Kim's love, even though she's not physically there. Diddy's reflections are often filled with gratitude for the time they had together, but also deep sorrow for the loss that continues to affect their family.

## Annual Celebrations and Keeping Her Memory Alive

Diddy has made it a priority to honor Kim Porter on important days, such as her birthday, Mother's Day, and the anniversary of her passing. Each year, he organizes family gatherings where they celebrate Kim's life. These moments are not just tributes but a way for the family to come together and keep her memory alive. He often shares these intimate celebrations on social media, giving the world a glimpse of how deeply Kim's absence is felt.

In 2020, on the second anniversary of her death, Diddy hosted a special tribute event with close family and friends. He shared pictures and videos of the gathering, which was filled with music, stories, and memories of Kim. The event was not only a way to mourn her loss but also to celebrate her life, as Diddy often emphasizes the importance of remembering the good times and the love she gave.

These annual celebrations are a reminder of how much Kim meant to Diddy and their family. Diddy's ongoing tributes and reflections show that, for him, Kim will always be a part of his life. Her influence remains strong, not only through their children but also in how Diddy continues to live his life, guided by the lessons she taught him.

## A Legacy of Love

In all of Diddy's tributes and reflections, one thing is clear: Kim Porter's legacy is defined by love. Whether it's through his public tributes, private reflections, or how he raises their children, Diddy's ongoing admiration for Kim shows the depth of their connection. He continues to celebrate her life and ensure that her spirit lives on through their family. For

Diddy, Kim will always be remembered as a woman who gave everything to her family, and her memory continues to guide him every day.

# The Lasting Influence Kim Porter Had on the Fashion and Entertainment Industries

Kim Porter's impact on both the fashion and entertainment industries went beyond her public appearances and high-profile relationships. She became a symbol of grace, resilience, and beauty, and her influence was felt in every project she touched, from the modelling shoots she took part into the music industry events she supported behind the scenes. Her influence continues to resonate, especially in the areas of diversity, beauty standards, and her role as a behind-the-scenes contributor to one of the most influential figures in music. This chapter will explore how Kim Porter's legacy shaped these industries and how her presence still reverberates today.

### Pioneering Diversity in Fashion

Kim Porter entered the modelling world during a time when diversity in fashion was not as prevalent as it is today. The industry was largely dominated by a narrow representation of beauty, particularly focusing on European standards. For a young Black woman from Georgia, breaking into this exclusive world required not only exceptional talent but also determination.

Kim's entrance into fashion showed the industry that beauty transcends race, and she became a role model for other aspiring Black models.

Her work with major brands and on magazine covers such as *Essence* put her in the spotlight and showcased the beauty of Black women. Her presence on these platforms paved the way for future generations of models of color, opening doors that had previously been difficult to walk through. The visibility Kim brought to women of color in the modelling industry was significant, as it challenged the industry's conventional beauty standards and contributed to the ongoing conversation about inclusion and representation.

Kim's success in modelling wasn't just about her physical beauty; it was also about the poise and confidence she carried with her. She made an impact not only because she was in front of the camera but because she presented herself with a level of class and dignity that set her apart. Younger models today still look to her as a trailblazer who fought to carve out a space for them in an industry that had historically overlooked them.

### Influence on Beauty Standards

Kim's beauty was not just skin-deep, and her influence on beauty standards went beyond her modelling career. As a woman of color, she represented a broader spectrum of beauty at a time when Black women were still fighting to see themselves in major fashion campaigns and magazines. Her presence in the fashion world challenged the industry to recognize the beauty of diversity and the power of representation.

She was an advocate for natural beauty, especially for women of color, promoting the idea that Black women did not need to conform to Eurocentric standards to be seen as beautiful. In a world where straightened hair, lighter skin, and specific facial features were often favored, Kim's embrace of her own natural beauty sent a strong message. Her confidence in who she was encouraged other women, especially Black women, to celebrate their own features without feeling pressured to alter them to fit into mainstream ideals.

Beyond the runway, Kim was deeply invested in the idea of self-care and wellness. She launched her own hair care line, **Three Brown Girls**, designed to cater to the unique needs of multicultural hair. This venture highlighted her commitment to empowering women to embrace their natural hair textures and take pride in who they were. Her influence in the beauty industry was about more than appearances; it was about instilling confidence in women to love themselves as they are. Today, many beauty brands and campaigns focus on inclusion, and Kim's advocacy for these values played a part in pushing the industry in that direction.

## Behind the Scenes in Entertainment

While many know Kim Porter for her high-profile relationship with Sean "Diddy" Combs, her role in the music and entertainment industries extended far beyond being a partner to a famous artist. Behind the scenes, Kim was a strong presence who supported Diddy and the artists around him. She was deeply involved in the creative process and often provided insight and guidance on projects.

Diddy himself often spoke of how integral Kim was to his career, referring to her as his "muse" and his rock. She was more than a partner—she was a confidante who had a strong understanding of the entertainment world and was able to offer valuable advice. Her ability to navigate the complex social and business dynamics of the industry allowed her to make a significant impact behind the scenes, whether through helping Diddy make critical decisions or offering support to artists in their creative endeavors.

Her influence wasn't always in the public eye, but it was felt by those who worked closely with her. Her presence at major music events and industry gatherings helped solidify her role as someone who was not just there for appearances but was truly involved in the creative and business aspects of the industry. This kind of influence, while subtle, was crucial in shaping some of the biggest moments in music history during the time she was active.

## A Role Model for Future Generations

Kim Porter's influence on both the fashion and entertainment industries left an enduring legacy that can be seen in the careers of many women today. She was a role model for women who sought to balance the demands of a high-profile career with the responsibilities of motherhood, showing that it was possible to succeed in both areas without compromising one for the other. Her ability to navigate the challenges of fame while staying grounded in her personal values inspired countless women to pursue their dreams with confidence.

Her legacy as a mother also plays a significant role in the entertainment industry today. Her children, Quincy, Christian, and twins D'Lila Star and Jessie James, have all gone on to pursue careers in music, fashion, and acting. They carry forward their mother's influence, embodying the values she instilled in them—hard work, humility, and the importance of staying true to oneself. Through them, Kim's influence continues to shape the industry, as they honor her memory and the lessons she taught them.

Kim's ability to maintain her identity while navigating a world filled with challenges set a powerful example for others. She showed that it was possible to succeed in industries that often push individuals to compromise their values. In doing so, she left a lasting influence on both fashion and entertainment, proving that beauty, strength, and integrity can coexist and create a legacy.


Kim Porter's influence on the fashion and entertainment industries cannot be overstated. As a model, she helped redefine beauty standards and opened doors for future generations of women of color. In entertainment, she was a supportive figure behind the scenes, offering insight and guidance that helped shape some of the most iconic moments in music. Her legacy continues to inspire, both through her work and through the lives of her children, who carry forward her values and passion. Her influence is one that will be remembered for years to come, as her grace, beauty, and strength continue to inspire those who follow in her footsteps.

# CONCLUSION

Kim Porter's life was marked by love, grace, and an enduring legacy that touched all who knew her. From her early days in Georgia to her success in the entertainment and fashion industries, Kim's journey was one of resilience, strength, and kindness. At the heart of it all was her unwavering devotion to her family and friends, her passion for making a positive impact, and her ability to remain grounded despite the spotlight that followed her.

Her role as a mother was central to her life. Raising four children—Quincy, Christian, and twins D'Lila Star and Jessie James—was Kim's greatest joy. She approached motherhood with the same grace and dedication that she brought to everything she did. Despite the fame and public attention surrounding her, she was determined to keep her children grounded. She instilled in them the values of humility, hard work, and compassion. Kim's presence in her children's lives wasn't just as a caregiver, but as a guide who wanted them to be strong individuals. Her legacy as a mother is reflected in the way her children speak of her today, full of love and admiration for the woman who shaped them.

Family always came first for Kim, but she also extended her love and support to those around her. Her friends often spoke of her loyalty, describing her as someone who would always show up, no matter how busy her life became. Whether it was offering advice, being a shoulder to lean on, or simply sharing a quiet moment of joy, Kim's friendships were rooted in deep connection and trust. She cultivated relationships that lasted for years, with many of her friends considering her family.

The people closest to Kim frequently noted her kindness and generosity. She had a way of making others feel special, valued, and loved. This wasn't limited to her personal relationships—Kim carried these traits into her professional life as well. She was often described as the person who quietly supported those around her, whether it was encouraging young models in the fashion industry or lending an ear to artists navigating the complexities of the music world. She didn't seek attention for her acts of kindness, but they left a lasting impression on those fortunate enough to experience them.

In addition to her personal qualities, Kim Porter left a significant mark on the entertainment industry. Her modelling career, which began in the 1990s, was one of the ways she first stepped into the public eye. She worked with major brands and appeared on magazine covers, showcasing not only her beauty but also her ability to bring grace and elegance to every project. Kim's work helped pave the way for greater diversity in fashion, especially for Black women. Her presence in the industry inspired others, and even though she eventually shifted her focus to family life, her contributions remained influential.

Kim's connection to the music world was undeniable. As the longtime partner of Sean "Diddy" Combs, she was a constant presence in the industry. While she wasn't directly involved in producing or performing, her support behind the scenes was deeply felt. She was a source of encouragement for Diddy, especially during difficult times, such as the loss of his close friend, the rapper Notorious B.I.G. Kim's quiet strength and ability to provide emotional support helped those around her navigate both personal and professional challenges.

Kim's entrepreneurial ventures also reflected her desire to empower others. With the launch of her unisex hair care line, **Three Brown Girls**, she aimed to create products that catered to the unique needs of multicultural hair. This business wasn't just about beauty; it was about helping women feel confident and seen. Kim believed in the power of self-expression and the importance of embracing one's natural beauty. Her brand carried that message forward, and it resonated with many women who appreciated her approach.

Her influence, of course, extended far beyond her professional achievements. When Kim Porter passed away in 2018, the outpouring of love and tributes from her friends, family, and colleagues was overwhelming. Those who knew her spoke not just of her accomplishments, but of her heart. Diddy, who had remained close to her despite their romantic relationship ending years earlier, described her as his best friend and the person who had always been there for him. The tributes from her children were especially poignant, as they shared how much they missed her presence in their lives and how deeply they felt her love, even after her passing.

The world mourned the loss of Kim Porter, but her legacy continues to live on through her children, her friends, and the countless people whose lives she touched. Her son, Quincy, has gone on to build a career in acting, carrying with him the lessons his mother taught him about grace and resilience. Christian, who has followed in his father's footsteps with a career in music and fashion, often speaks about how his mother's influence helped shape his path. The twins, D'Lila and Jessie, are growing up in an environment filled with the love and values Kim instilled in them, and they, too, are finding their own voices in the world.

Diddy's ongoing tributes to Kim reflect the deep connection they shared. He continues to honor her memory in interviews, social media posts, and family events, making sure that Kim's spirit remains an integral part of their lives. He has spoken about how her love continues to guide him as a father and how he strives to uphold the values she lived by.

Kim Porter's life was defined by the love she gave and the grace with which she carried herself. She touched people in ways that went far beyond her public persona. Her legacy is one of strength, kindness, and an unwavering commitment to the people she loved. As those who knew her reflect on her life, they remember a woman who was as beautiful on the inside as she was on the outside, someone who brought light into every room she entered. Her memory continues to inspire others to live with the same love and grace that she embodied every day.

In the end, Kim Porter's story is a reminder of the power of love, the importance of family, and the impact one person can have on the lives of so many.

Her life was cut short, but the legacy she left behind will endure for generations to come.

# Appendix

# Tributes and Memories

Kim Porter's life touched countless people, and the outpouring of love and respect after her passing demonstrated the depth of her impact. Family, friends, and colleagues all spoke of her warmth, strength, and unwavering love for her children. This section brings together some of the heartfelt tributes from those who knew her best. These memories serve as a lasting testament to the woman she was and the legacy she left behind.

Sean "Diddy" Combs, who shared a long and deeply connected relationship with Kim, was one of the first to speak out after her passing. Diddy often described Kim as his "best friend" and "soulmate," a woman who stood by his side through life's ups and downs. Reflecting on the mother of his children, Diddy shared that Kim was a pillar of strength in their family. He expressed how much he admired her ability to nurture their children while maintaining grace and poise in the public eye. He once said, "I miss you so much. We were more than soulmates. We were some other shit! And I miss you so much. I know you're with us still, and you'll always be in my heart. I love you forever."

Kim's children, Quincy, Christian, and the twins, D'Lila Star and Jessie James, often remember their mother as their greatest source of love and encouragement. Quincy, her eldest son, expressed his gratitude for everything his mother instilled in him. In one of his most emotional tributes, Quincy spoke of his mother's unwavering support and how she always believed in him, no matter the challenges he faced. He shared, "There wasn't a day that went by when I didn't feel her love. She made sure I knew that I could do anything I put my mind to. My mother was my biggest cheerleader."

Christian, often following in his father's footsteps, mentioned that his mother always encouraged him to chase his dreams. He once reflected on how Kim helped him balance the demands of growing up in the spotlight while staying grounded in family values. Christian said, "She was my first teacher. She taught me to be proud of who I am, to always lead with love, and to take care of my family." He often refers to his mother as the guiding light in his life, someone who always knew the right words to say and who could bring comfort during tough times.

D'Lila and Jessie, though younger, shared a close bond with their mother. Friends and family often talk about how Kim adored her daughters, making sure they were loved and cared for every moment of the day. While the girls have been more private, those close to the family speak of how Kim's presence is still felt in their lives. Even at a young age, they often talk about how they feel their mother's spirit with them every day. They remember her as their protector, someone who always put them first and showered them with love.

Mary J. Blige, one of Kim's closest friends, was among the many who publicly mourned her loss. Mary described Kim as "one of the realest people" she had ever known, praising her for always staying true to herself despite the pressures of the entertainment industry. Mary said, "Kim was so special, and you always knew where you stood with her. She was never afraid to be honest, and that's something I loved about her. She had this amazing way of making you feel like family." Kim and Mary shared a deep bond, supporting each other through various challenges in their careers and personal lives. Their friendship was built on mutual respect, and Kim's passing left a significant void in Mary's life.

Beyoncé, another close friend of Kim's, also paid tribute to her. She shared a touching post honoring Kim's grace and love for her children, describing her as "the epitome of strength and love." Beyoncé reflected on how Kim was a woman who balanced her role as a mother and public figure with unmatched dignity. She often admired Kim's ability to remain strong and present for her family, even when the world around her demanded so much. In her tribute, Beyoncé said, "Kim's love for her children was her greatest gift. She was their everything, and she did it all with so much grace."

Longtime friend Naomi Campbell also shared her grief, expressing how Kim's loss impacted those who knew her best. Naomi, who had known Kim for years, often spoke of her beauty and grace, both inside and out. She said, "Kim was a queen, a true example of what it means to be a strong, loving woman. She always made sure the people around her felt her love and support." Naomi reflected on the memories they shared together, from fashion shows to private moments, saying that Kim's presence brought light into every room she entered.

Kim's ability to form deep, meaningful connections extended beyond the celebrity circle. Her friends and loved ones from her hometown in Georgia also shared fond memories of her. Many spoke of how Kim never forgot her roots, often visiting Columbus and maintaining lifelong friendships with people she grew up with. A childhood friend shared, "Kim was always down to earth. No matter how much success she found, she never forgot where she came from. She had a heart of gold, and she treated everyone with kindness."

One of Kim's close family members remarked on how she was the glue that held everyone together. Family gatherings were always important to Kim, and she made it a priority to stay connected to her extended family. The family member reflected, "Kim was the heart of our family. She always brought everyone together, whether it was for holidays or just a regular Sunday dinner. She made sure that we stayed close and supported each other."

Throughout her life, Kim Porter was known for her authenticity, kindness, and dedication to the people she loved. Whether through her role as a mother, a friend, or a mentor, Kim's influence reached far beyond her immediate circle. Her passing left a void that has been felt by many, but her legacy of love and strength continues to shine through the memories of those who were fortunate enough to know her.

This collection of tributes is just a glimpse into the many lives Kim touched. Her warmth, compassion, and unwavering dedication to her family and friends remain her greatest legacy, reminding everyone of the profound impact one person can have on the world around them.

Made in the USA
Las Vegas, NV
26 September 2024

95806527R00069